He was there All The Time

Book Cover Page 5, 28, 106

He was there All The Time

- Joyce H. Jones

Outskirts Press, Inc.
Denver, Colorado

Contents

Dedication & Acknowledgement

This book is dedicated to my very dear friend Josephine, whom I loved like a sister. I pray this book will announce to the world that her living was not in vain. It may have taken some time for her to accept and love her fellow man but it is always better to be late than never. I would like to acknowledge her beautiful spirit and her zeal for life. After she became a Christian, she would give you her last dime to help if you were in need of something. If you knew her, you would certainly love her. I know she is in heaven with the Father looking down upon us saying, "Look at those crazy people." I want the world to know that she was here; she made her contribution to the world as the Lord had ordained it and then she left.

I want to thank God for giving me the privilege of telling my friend's story as best I can. I know it will certainly touch the hearts of anyone who reads this testimony. This book will make a statement of her life here on earth and she will be remembered as one of God's chosen.

Introduction

When I think about the different people God has placed in my path during my lifetime, it saddens me to see how I missed the mark. I missed the mark because I was focusing on un-forgiveness and sin. I walked right by the people who could have changed my direction but I was unable to recognize goodness or Godly people at the time. When the Lord finally opened my eyes to his goodness, I was able to see the people God was sending my way to minister to and care for me. One of the main things I noticed was that God did not always send someone of your race to minister to you. I. believed that I could only receive things such as love and affection from people of my own race but I have found this not to be true. For instance, two of the most important men in my life today are a Jew and an Irishman. God has proven to me that race is not important and that we are all sisters and brothers in his eyes. I told those two people in my life that I know God placed me with them and that God has a sense of humor because only he would send a black woman to a Jew and an Irishman to care for each other. This book is to glorify God for his love and protection over my girlfriend's life. God allowed her to live her life the way she wanted to live it because he gave us all free will. At the age of seven her free will took her into the wilderness. No one taught her right from wrong; therefore, she followed the path that she thought was right. Unfortunately, the path she took was the path that led to hell.

At the age of 47 she received her salvation and Jesus led her out of the wilderness for good. She gave up alcohol, drugs, adultery, fornication, stealing, and everything else bad that you can think of; however, she kept going back into the wilderness because she could not give up the hate and un-forgiveness toward those who had abused and neglected her when she was a child. She felt that someone had to pay for the pain, suffering, and humiliation that had been forced upon her during her childhood. It didn't matter that all the people who had hurt her were dead. The pain and suffering was still alive in her heart and she could not let go of them.

Un-forgiveness was her lifeline, it kept her alive.

As long as she held onto un-forgiveness she felt that she could blame someone else for her sinful behavior. God forgave her of her sins June 8, 1994, but she was not ready to forgive those who had sinned against her. Nevertheless, God had other plans for her that she was not aware of.

Prologue

On October 13, 1998, while dreaming, she heard a loud voice say to her, "Look up." When she looked up she saw a narrow road that led to heaven. Next to the road was a cross and next to the cross was the face of a man whom she believed to be Jesus. The voice in the dream said, "This is the end of the road." At that point she began to plead with the other people in her dream to "look up." No one would look up and it seemed that everyone ignored her. She fell to her knees and began to pray. She said, "Lord, forgive me; please forgive me of my sins." Repeatedly she kept saying the same thing over and over again. The voice in the dream said, "Stop it! You are just praying so that the people can see you. You do not really mean what you are saying." Then the voice said, "You have one year to live."

When she woke up she thought about 2 Peter 3:8:

"But, beloved, be not ignorant of this one thing, that one day with the Lord is as a thousand years, and a thousand years as one day." (KJV) While thinking about this, she became very fearful because she thought she was going to die right away. She said, "Lord, am I going to die today?" She waited for an answer but received no response. Still waiting for an answer she fell back to sleep and began to dream the same dream all over again. In the second dream she was given some instructions as to what she needed to do to prepare for the return of Jesus. She knew in her heart that she had only provided "lip service forgiveness" to people whom she felt had wronged her. She had spoken forgiveness out of her mouth but it did not come from her heart. She was ashamed because she taught others about God's word. (Matt 18:35 KJV) "Likewise shall your heavenly Father do also unto you, if ye from your heart forgive not every one his brother their trespasses." (You really need to read verses 21 through 35) She had failed to abide by the words she was teaching. She knew it was going to be a struggle to let go of the un-forgiveness because her hardened heart had been formed in childhood. She had learned at an early age to live without love. The bitterness of thinking about what she had been through as a child and knowing that no one really cared about her was unforgivable. The question she had to ask herself was, "How can I forgive someone that I don't love?" The answer to this question and all questions can be found in the Bible. Matthew 6:14 "For if ye forgive men their trespasses, your heavenly Father will also forgive you."

Not loving the people whom she felt had wronged her as a child was Satan's last stronghold on her. The Spirit of God was the only power that could relieve her of this burden that she had been carrying around for most of her life. After giving her situation much thought she began to cry out to God. She said, *Prayer* "Father, deliver me from the un-forgiveness and pain in my heart. Create in me a clean heart, O God; and renew a right spirit within me." (Psalms 51:10 KJV) "Father, I am so ashamed of the life I have lived. I know that you have forgiven me but I have not forgiven those who have wronged me. I am ashamed for disobeying your word. Your word commands us to forgive those who have wrongfully used us. I thank you for having patience with me. It is an honor to know that you, God Almighty, took the time to walk with me and hold my hand. You protected me when my mother placed me in an unsafe home. You watched over me and kept me through alcohol and drug abuse. You have walked with me throughout my sinful life. You never left me, nor did you allow me to leave you, even though I walked away from you several times. God, I do not deserve your grace, mercy, or love; however, I thank you for it. I thank you for giving me another chance. I thank you for allowing me to show others that you are a God who holds onto his children. God, I ask you to allow this book to be a blessing to everyone who reads it. I pray that your Holy Spirit will arrest anyone reading this book who needs to be delivered or set free and that you show forth your love toward them as it has been demonstrated in these pages.

"Let your love, forgiveness, and deliverance show in every word and every testimony. Unto you God, I give all glory for my life and my strength. In Jesus' name I pray, Amen."

Chapter 1
MY PERCEPTIONS AND
THE DEVIL'S DECEPTION

For as long as I can remember my mother would give me away to anyone who would take me. I thought it was normal for mothers to give away their children. I did everything I could to try to get my mother to keep me; however, nothing I did pleased her. It was my perception that if I was obedient, my mother would not give me away. I quickly learned that being obedient was not what it took for my mother to keep me. At some point I began to believe that if I was bad (deception) I could win my mother's love. I assumed that if she loved me she would not give me away.

I was ashamed of my mother because she drank alcohol. However, her drinking was not the issue. What mattered to me more than anything else was that I wanted to be with her because she was the only family I knew. One day I asked my mother a question that changed my life forever, and it also changed my way of thinking. My mother and I were going to visit my brother, who was in jail for stealing. I asked her to give me some of the peanuts she had bought for him. She said, "These peanuts are for your brother."

"Why can't I have some? I'm a good girl. He's bad, that's why he's in jail."

My mother had previously told me that jail was for bad people. I assumed my brother was a bad person because he was in jail. She said, "I am taking him peanuts because I love him." After that day, I wanted to be like my brother. My brother was a thief, yet my mother still loved him. I wanted that same love so I started stealing too. The only problem with stealing was when I got caught my mother would whip me. The more I stole, the more she whipped me. It took me a while to realize that stealing was not the way to make her happy.

Chapter 2
IT'S TIME TO GO

"Get up, baby sister, it's time to go." I dreaded the tone and the sound of those words because I knew that in getting up, this could be one of those days that my mother would give me away again. Moving slowly around the one-room dwelling where my mother and I lived, I obeyed and got dressed. Although I tried to be a good little girl, I was never obedient enough to stop my mother from giving me away. As I was getting dressed I was thinking, "Why can't she see that I don't want to go? Can't she see I love her? Doesn't she understand I'm afraid?" I did everything my mom told me to do. I even got dressed to go somewhere I didn't want to go just to please her. I waited by the door with my little brown bag, which contained bread. I always had bread in a brown bag. Each day I would go from house to house in the neighborhood to get bread from the neighbors. It was not that my mother didn't feed me. This was my way of getting attention.

My mother and I walked about a block to the train station. By the time we arrived there, a lady was waiting for us. The lady and my mother talked for a few minutes. I did not hear what they were talking about so I started to play on the train tracks. The next thing I remember was my mother walking away. I started to follow her but the lady stopped me. She said, "You are going with me!" As I watched my mother walk away, all I could think of was that she didn't even tell me good-bye. I watched her, hoping she would look back just once, but of course she didn't. She didn't even stop to contemplate turning around. I was afraid, but I did not cry. As she walked away I lost all hope of ever being loved. I can still remember how I hated her and loved her at the same time. I loved her because she was all I had, but I hated her for giving me away.

As I walked along with the person whom I did not want to be with, I was thinking about how I could get her to give me back to my mother. I had been though this procedure before and I knew the drill. If I made the people whom I was given to mad enough they would give me back to my mother. My mind was working overtime trying to figure out what I could do to make this new lady give me back. As we entered the person's house I saw the answer lying right there on the floor. It was a big, fat brown cat on the side of the entrance of the house. I hated cats and I had no intention of living with this one.

The next day I gathered all the children I had met in the neighborhood and told them I wanted them to help me kill the cat. I informed them that if they told anyone, or if they did not help me kill the cat, I would kill them. This was the beginning of the destructive and controlling life I led for over 40 years. God showed me a vision of the day my mother left me. He showed me that Jesus was holding my hand while I was standing there on the train track. I believed what God had shown me, but I also believed that somewhere along the line Satan took control of my mind. I know it was the devil who gave me the idea and the power to control the children and force them to kill that cat. When the person I was living with asked me if I had seen the cat, I told her I had killed it. She looked at me and said, "You are evil." I was proud of what I had done. I wanted her to give me back to my mother. I just knew I would be on my way back home to my mother real soon.

Chapter 3
GOD'S PROTECTION

My plan had worked perfectly. When the lady took me back to my mother, Mom did not waste any time finding another place for me to live. The only problem with the new home was that danger waited at the door for me. In this home, a man attempted to molest me. He gave me a nickel to let him lie on me. I took the nickel, but something (I now know it was the Holy Spirit) told me what the man was doing was wrong. God's Spirit told me that I was in danger. The Spirit told me to "go next door to the store and tell the store-owner what the man wants you to do." I told the man I would let him lie on me if he would let me get a soda first. When this incident occurred I had no idea who or what God was; however, I know now that he was there protecting me. I tricked the man into believing me because he agreed to let me go. I ran from the house, hoping my mother would come and get me. I informed the owner of the store what the man was trying to do. The store-owner called my mother. She informed my mother that if she did not take me out of that house she would have her arrested. When I left the store I was so afraid. I didn't really understand what the man was trying to do, but I knew it was wrong.

I went back to the house, but instead of going inside I hid under the house. When I saw my mother I ran to her. I was so glad to see her. My mother looked at me but did not say anything. She looked so sad. I believed the sad look on her face meant that she did not love me nor want me. I was nine years old when this happened. Forty-three years later I can still feel the pain that I felt on that day. My mother was a beautiful, statuesque woman, but that day she looked very small and helpless. I was sad too because I felt I had made her sad.

During the first ten years of my life, my mother gave me away to five different families. Most of the people were decent, but I was so evil they could not control me. It did not matter to me that they would provide for me well, buy me nice clothes, and have plenty of food for me to eat. I didn't care how well they treated me; I only wanted to be with my mother.

I did whatever I felt had to be done to be with her. After my mother took me home for the fifth time, about two weeks later, she died.

When I arrived home from school on October 31, 1956, my mother was not there. As it began to get dark, I could feel the rage building up inside of me. I don't know how long it took me to reach the breaking point, but, all of a sudden, I started breaking and destroying everything in sight. After I had destroyed everything in the house that I could destroy, I walked over to my cousin's house. Around two o'clock that morning, I heard my cousin say to someone on the phone, "Everyone has to die sometime." I don't know how, but I knew my mother was dead. I was not sad nor did I cry. I was thinking, what am I going to do now? The next day my cousin told me that my mother had died in jail. She said the policeman found her on the street drunk. We later discovered that she had a stroke and the policeman had refused to take her to the hospital. When my cousin went to the house where we lived she was shocked. She said, "What happened here?" I said, "I don't know, maybe someone broke in." I felt good because I had gotten away with another lie. Satan has a way of making you feel really good about sin. When my mother died, I was relieved because I believed I was finally going to have a real home.

The only problem I now had was going back to school. It made me sick to even think what the children were going to do and say to me. God took control of the situation. When I went back to school, no one said anything to me about my mother. God shielded me from the pain and embarrassment of my mother dying in jail.

For most of my life, I have blamed my mother for placing me in danger. However, during the writing of this book, God has shown me that my mother had no way of knowing I would be in danger. God has also shown me that he was always there to protect me. I came to believe that my mother did not neglect me but was trying to make sure I would be taken care of (because she knew that she couldn't do it herself). God has allowed me to leave the prison (hell, wilderness) that held me in bondage for so many years. For all those years Satan had tricked me into believing that my mother did not want me. John 8:32: "Then you will know the truth, and the truth will set you free."

Now that I am free, I can understand why during my entire life I have never been able to truly love anyone. I had to first forgive and love my mother, and then I could feel love for or give love to others.

Prior to the writing of this book, whenever I thought of my mother I had only two emotions—pain and un-forgiveness. I now know what it is like to feel the love of a mother. God has shown me how to love my mother even though she is no longer with me. (Forgiveness is the key.) Satan had deceived me into thinking my mother did not love me. He stole all of the good memories of my mother away from me. However, little by little, God has shown me the beauty of the woman he chose as the vessel to bring me into this world. Presently, I can only remember my mother's back as she walked away from me. But I know that one day God is going to allow me to re-member and see her face. I can only remember her whipping me. However, I believe God is going to show me a vision of her hugging me. I cannot re-member her ever touching me except to whip me when I cursed or stole something.

Chapter 4
WHAT DO WE DO WITH THIS CHILD?

After my mother's death, a decision had to be made about what to do with the little devil, Josephine. No one wanted me because I was evil. The decision was made to give me to the first person who would take me. I was given to a nice family who lived in the country. This family would have been the ideal situation; unfortunately, it was too late for me. I did not know how to live and behave like a normal child anymore. I didn't have any friends at my new school because I was so mean no one wanted to play with me. The children made fun of me because I did not have a mother or father. I knew I had to take control of my new situation. I had to get some friends. I felt that if I had something to offer, I could buy some friends. I needed money so I began to steal again. Stealing always came easy for me. It was as if I was gifted in this area.

In the home I lived in, the man of the house was sick. He always kept large amounts of cash in his pockets. Every other morning before going to school, while he slept I would take money from his pockets. I would buy candy and give it to the children I wanted to play with. It did not take long for me to have as many friends as I wanted. My stealing and buying candy lasted about four months. The man from the store where I bought the candy had seen me come in with the lady of the house. One day when I came in with her, he told her I had been spending large amounts of money buying candy. It did not take her long to figure out where I was getting the money from. She did not waste any time getting me packed up and then taking me back to my cousin.

Chapter 5
FOLLOWING THE PAST

When I think about the different people God has placed in my path during my lifetime, it saddens me to see how I missed the mark. I missed the mark because I was focusing on un-forgiveness and sin. I walked right by the people who could have changed my direction, but I was unable to recognize goodness or godly people at the time. When I finally opened my eyes I was able to see the people God was sending my way to minister to and care for me. One of the main things I noticed is that God did not always send someone of your race or color to minister to you. I believed that I could only receive things such as love and affection from people of my own race, but I have found this not to be true.

Sidebar: I think I should mention right

here that Josey was married to a German man while she was stationed in Germany. She told me she married him so that she could get additional money from the government in the form of separate rations and Basic Allowance for Quarters. She also told me that her husband promised to buy her a Mercedes-Benz if she married him. Well, sure enough, Josey drove proudly in her brown Mercedes. I am not sure if she sold the car when she left Germany or if she brought it with her to Texas and sold it there. She told me she was ashamed of him and refused to go out with him anywhere. She did not love him when they first married, but she did grow to love him after she gave her life to the Lord. Her prayer was that one day she and her husband would reunite. She did not have a male friend that I know of. She told me she would never cheat on her husband, even though they were not together. She did tell me that she liked the Jewish man and that he liked her. Whenever he went on trips he would always bring her back a gift. She even went out to dinner with him once, but I think that was as far as that relationship went.

Chapter 6
COUSIN MARY

Cousin Mary was an unfeeling person who did not give or accept love. At times she was very cruel. When I was placed back in her care I knew I had made a big mistake. I begged the family to take me back, but they refused because they said they could never trust me again. Thus, I began my life with my cousin, who abused me for approximately five years while I lived with her. She abused me mentally but not physically. The first time she hit me I hit her back and ran away. I slept under the house that night with the chickens. The next day I reported her to the welfare office. I begged the welfare representative to send me to another foster home. They told me they would have to put me into a home for girls and I would have to stay there until I was 18. I didn't want to live with my cousin; however, I did not want to stay in a girls' home until I was 18 either. I told the representative from the welfare office that I would stay with my cousin, but if she hit me again I would run away. My cousin promised the people from the welfare office that she would never hit me again. After this incident my cousin punished me whenever I did something she did not like. She didn't beat me because she thought I was crazy and would fight her back.

Somehow, violence became a part of my life after my mother's death. I felt I had to defend myself against the world. I had to control my life and the people in charge of me. For instance, I made it clear to everyone if they hit me, I would hit them back. The first teacher who hit me after my mother died got his face slapped. I was expelled from school and my cousin told the teachers at the school that I was crazy. My cousin told the teacher to send me home and she would punish me there. I believe she got a great deal of joy punishing me. To give you an example of this, there was only one bed in our home; therefore, I was forced to sleep with her. I was not allowed to move once I got in bed. If my movement caused her to wake up she would yell at me and call me names. I would lie in bed every night afraid to move. There is no way to explain this type of fear. It grips your entire body and overtakes you. The closest thing I can think of would be Russian roulette. Someone places the gun next to your head and you wait for the gun to go off. That is how the game was played. I would lie in fear night after night afraid to go to sleep, thinking I might move in my sleep. Eventually someone gave my cousin a cot for me to sleep on. The cot made noise when I moved, but I learned how to turn over without her hearing me.

To add to the nightly abuse, there was the daily humiliation I was forced to endure. During the winter season I was forced to wash clothes outside in the freezing cold. Sometimes it was so cold the water would freeze before I was through washing. I can remember how cold my hands would get. I would try to hurry, but I could not take the chance of the clothes not being clean. Many times the clothes would freeze while I was putting them on the line. As I stood there in the cold washing, I could feel the hate for my cousin and for the world rising up and growing even stronger inside me. Even as I write this book, I find myself frowning and wishing I could punish her for what she did to me.

After the clothes dried, it was my responsibility to iron them. If I left one wrinkle in her uniforms she would wet the whole dress and make me iron it over again.

Many times when she was not pleased with how I did the housework she would say, "You will never amount to anything. You are just like your mother and that no-good daddy of yours." Since I didn't know I had a daddy, I had no idea who she was talking about. When she would get on a roll degrading me, I would just look at her like she was crazy. She slapped my face once because she saw me looking down when a white woman was speaking to me. My cousin's words to me were, "Never look down when a white person speaks to you. You look them right in the face. This lets them know you are nobody's nigger and that you are not afraid of them." So when she would try to intimidate me, I would look her right in the face to let her know I was not her nigger and that she could not intimidate me. She hated it when I looked at her because she knew I didn't care what she said. When one type of punishment failed to work she would try something different. It was as if she was trying to break my spirit. What she did not know was that my mother had broken my spirit before she died.

Another one of her cruel game was, after school, she would make me sit on the porch and do my homework. She would turn my chair from the street and make me face the house while she watched me from the window. If I turned around, she would holler at me and say, "See, you never know when I'm watching." When the other children in the neighborhood finished their homework they would walk up and down the street mocking me. I would sit on the porch filled with anger because I couldn't look back to see who was making fun of me. There was only one girl who would play with me. However, I began to notice that when her light-skinned friends came over she no longer wanted to play with me. They would ask her why she was playing with that black girl. She would then tell me that I had to leave. One day I decided it was time to teach Betty a lesson. I took her to the woodshed and I beat her until she said I was her friend. After that she played with me whenever I wanted her to.

After living with my cousin for a year she informed me that a man would be moving in. I was afraid of men after the man had tried to molest (rape) me. My cousin's male friend made it clear that he did not want her to keep me. My cousin told me he wanted her to put me in a home for girls. She told him no one in our family had ever been put in a home for girls. I knew she was keeping me for the money the state was paying her for me to stay there. I was a child but I was wise. I knew about everything that was going on around me. I was very knowledgeable, but the knowledge I had acquired was not from God, it was from the devil. Satan made sure that I believed everyone hated me.

My cousin finally figured out a way to keep me and the man. She bought him liquor and then let him eat the food I was supposed to eat. I never went hungry, but the type of food I ate changed after he moved in. For instance, after he came, when my cousin cooked chicken I was only given the necks and backs. I had to wait until he ate before I could eat. I was not allowed to sit at the table until he had finished eating. I hated my cousin for giving him my food. I knew she used the money the state gave her to take care of me to buy the food he ate. As I sat and watched him eat, I felt like a dog waiting for the leftovers. I promised myself that when I grew up I would eat all the chicken I wanted, but I would never ever eat a back, neck, or wing. When I made this promise to myself I never knew that it would lead to an eating disorder.

When we make promises to ourselves that are not godly promises, we place a curse on our life. I told myself I would eat as much as I wanted when I got grown. When I left my cousin's house I started to eat and drink whatever I wanted, whenever I wanted it. The results of the childhood promises led to my becoming an alcoholic along with acquiring an eating disorder. Most of my friends knew I was an alcoholic, but no one knew I had an eating disorder. Many times I would eat so much it would make me sick. I was unable to stop eating. I had a spirit of gluttony upon me. When I finally told my friends about my problems, I was able to stop with the help of God. By the time I stopped I had already damaged my health. Only by the grace of God have I lived as long as I have. God has allowed me to outlive all of the females in my immediate family, even though I have abused this temple by disobeying him. Phil 3:19: "Whose end is destruction, whose god is their belly, and whose glory is in their shame, who mind earthly things."

Another promise I made was that I would have all the clothes I wanted. My desire to obtain clothes almost landed me in jail, but God and his grace protected me. My pastor always say that God will not bless you in your mess. This is true; nevertheless, God has allowed me to go though many trials for a testimony to glorify his name and to prove his love for me. The one thing to remember is: "Be not deceived; God is not mocked: for whatsoever a man soweth, that shall he also reap." (Galatians: 6:7 KJV)

My obsession to fulfill my childhood promises

almost destroyed my life. There were many times I sat in the parking lot of shopping centers trying with all my strength not to go into the stores and shop. I always lost. I went shopping every day. It did not matter what I bought. It did not matter if I needed what I bought. I just had to shop. Most of the things I bought were from the Goodwill stores. I would rationalize that it was okay to buy things as long as it was a good bargain. I would buy tables for two or three months; then I would buy lamps. I bought anything I felt was a bargain. During these periods I would try to understand why I could not control my obsessive need to shop. At some point I became afraid I would start stealing again if I did not have the money to buy what I wanted. God delivered me from this obsession after I confessed my sin to my friends. James 5:16 states: "Confess your faults one to another, and pray one for another, that ye may be healed. The effectual fervent prayer of a righteous man availeth much."(KJV)

Compulsive (an irresistible impulse to act irrationally) shopping and eating are sins when they are controlled by the devil (spirit of gluttony). The only way to prevent the devil from controlling you is to openly confess your sin. Once you expose him he will leave you alone for a period of time. James 4:7:

"Submit your selves, then, to God. Resist the devil, and he will flee from you. If he cannot conquer you in one area he will simply change his tactics and try another area. We must always remember that Satan has many strongholds. He has many ways of seducing us and tempting us. This is why Jesus taught us to pray and say: "Lead us not into temptation but deliver us from evil." Help us not to have more on us than we can bear. Keep us away from sin. Protect us from Satan. Let us not fall into sin and wallow there. God will give us the courage to get back up and start all over again.

Chapter 7
FROM STEALING TO DRUGS

During the time my brother lived with me, he became a drug pusher and I became a drug user. My brother never gave me any drugs. I would get the drugs from his girlfriend. He was not aware that I was taking drugs until one night I almost took an overdose of pills. I thought I was going to die. When I called my brother he came to my rescue as quickly as he could. The look on his face told me that I should be scared. He looked like he was going to kill me. He took me home from the hospital where I remained sick for three days. I promised my brother I would never take drugs again. This was another time where God stepped in to save my life. God prevented me from dying, but he did not stop me from getting sick. I did not use any more drugs until much later on in life. At this point I must stop and thank God because every time I took drugs they would make me sick and I would become out of control. I hated not being able to control my speech and my thoughts. I finally gave up because of the lack of control over my thoughts. My question to God was, "Why did you not let me enjoy the drugs I took? Why did you not let the drugs become a habit? Why didn't you let me die?" God's response is the same one he always gives: "Because I love you."

The vision that God showed me was of Jesus holding my hand when I was a child, and it would come to my memory when I thought about the drugs I used. I can only thank God for being there as I traveled down the road of destruction. Without him holding my hand I would have fallen. Every woman and most of the men in my family have died from some terrible disease or drugs, but God has allowed me to live. I have outlived all of the people in my family who said I would never amount to anything. Perhaps I have shortened my life by disobedience; nevertheless, I can say I made it this far. If I leave this world today or tomorrow I can say God allowed me to make it to a point in my life where I tried to love everybody. I thank Him for not allowing me to leave this world with un-forgiveness and vengeance in my heart.

Sidebar: While we were talking about stealing, Josey told me how the enemy had instructed her on how to steal and not get caught. She had very large breasts and could stick things down in her bra without any-one knowing it. Any small item she wanted would easily fit between her cleavage. One other way she got money was to go into a well-known chain store, steal merchandise from that store, but take it to another store to receive a refund. Back in those days in high-class stores no one would question you if you returned merchandise. You cannot get away with that tactic these days; the most you can get without a receipt is a store credit. She would have hundreds of dollars in her purse but would steal the item she wanted anyway. At that point it was not about the money. She said it made her feel powerful to steal some-thing and not get caught. We talked about many ways she stole things, but she did not want to teach people, who did not steal be-cause they were afraid they would get caught, how to steal and get away with it.

Chapter 8
ON MY OWN

After I finished high school I moved to New Jersey. Once I was on my own, I began to act like my mother and my cousin. I began to do all the things I hated about them. I started to drink alcohol like a fish, curse like a sailor, and eat everything I wanted, like food was going out of style. I was determined to make up for all the food I missed eating as a child. My goal was to eat all the chicken in the state of New Jersey. Every time I thought about my cousin's boyfriend eating the chicken that should have been given to me, I would get angry. I never dreamed that it was destroying my body. My stomach became my God. Phil 3:19: "Whose end is destruction, whose God is their belly, and whose glory is in their shame, who mind earthly things." (KJV)

Parents and caregivers do not realize how little

things said or done to a child can influence or destroy their life. Overeating was my way of getting back at my cousin. Jesus taught that we should love our enemies. Luke 6:27: "But I say unto you which hear, love your enemies, do good to them which hate you." The more I ate the better I felt. I was deceived into thinking I was doing the right thing.

The first week in New Jersey I became involved with a married man. I was seventeen years old and I thought the man loved me. I was very happy because I believed I had finally found someone who really loved me. He told me he was going to leave his wife so that he could be with me all the time. I believed him at first; then after a year, I began to realize he was lying just so he could get what he wanted from me. He told me his wife would not give him a divorce. I was so young and inexperienced I believed all the lies he told me about his wife. She finally came to see me. They had two small children. She told me she had known about her husband and me for a long time. She also knew I was not aware of the fact that Alex was not feeding his family. He was giving me most of his money. When I looked at her and the children I thought about how I had been denied food when I was a child. I knew what it was like not to have a father or someone to care for you. Right then and there I asked her to forgive me. She was a very nice lady who had a jerk for a husband. She thanked me for listening to her. When Alex came home that night I told him about my life before meeting him. I begged him to go back to his wife and told him that I would not be seeing him anymore. I found out later on that he and his wife were very happy together, so everything worked out great.

As I think about it now, I didn't care about the wife at all. It was the children I was concerned about. Allowing the man who I thought loved me to go back to his wife and children was hard but I did it. I could not live with him or myself knowing that I was taking the food out of his children's mouths. That was a very hard pill to swallow. As I think back on that incident, I believe that was my first act of kindness.

About two years after I moved to New Jersey my brother, the thief, came to live with me. This was probably the worst thing that could have happened to me. My brother trained me how to be a professional thief. I am not proud of the things I did because of him, but I did them anyway.

At this point, I need to make it clear that I am not boasting when I use the words professional thief; nevertheless, a professional thief was what I became. For example: I was once caught stealing merchandise from a store. I was sent to the police station and thoroughly searched, but, as usual, I got away clean. I was in control of that situation because by that time in my life, I was so controlled and led by the devil I thought I could get away with anything. When the policewoman began to search me I would attack her sense of pride and humility. I knew I had to take control of the situation or else I would be caught red-handed. I had the merchandise on me, so I could not allow her to search me and find it. I (with the thoughts placed in my head by Satan) came up with a way to intimidate her. When she touched me I would ask her things like, "Do you enjoy your job? Are you gay? Are you getting off by feeling and touching me?" Once I realized she was getting upset about what I was saying, I knew I had found her weakness.

Being a woman myself, I know that if you are not gay you do not want to be called nor implied to be gay. I told her when she touched me it made me feel dirty. I was as cruel and nasty as I could be to her. I wanted to make her loathe her job so much that she would not want to search me in certain places. She told me to shut up, but I kept right on talking. Each time she attempted to touch me I would ask her if it felt good for her to touch me. She would spontaneously back away from me. That is just what I wanted her to do. I think she believed I was the devil. To make a long story short, I walked out of the police station with the items I had stolen, and the video on which they had caught me stealing was erased. No one knew how the tape was erased, not even me, but I sure was glad the proof they thought they had against me was no longer there. I walked away from what should have been a embarrassing situation; however, I was not embarrassed at all. I was well pleased with myself.

I should have let the matter drop, but when you are being controlled and driven by Satan, nothing you do is ever enough. Satan will destroy you and help you to destroy everyone and everything around you if you allow him to. My next step was to charge the person who caught me with slander. I accused her of targeting me because I was black. Before the case was over, I had convinced the store owners, the lawyer, and everyone involved that I was just a poor black woman who was treated unfairly. The person who caught me lost her job. The sad thing about the whole situation is she was good at her job but got punished for doing the job she was paid to do. I know she was good because she caught me. I had stolen from this store for four years. Stealing is similar to taking drugs; the more you steal, the more you want to steal. Each time you get away with it, your desire becomes stronger. The only problem with stealing is you will eventually be caught. The reason I was caught was greed. I would go from one post-exchange store to the other and steal. I would steal an item at one place and carry it back to another store without a receipt and request a refund. It was so easy because everyone basically went with the honor system on a military base unless they suspected foul play. I didn't need the money. I just enjoyed doing it.

After I was almost caught, I stopped stealing. Can you believe I later became a security guard in a department store? My job as a security guard was to catch shoplifters. (What a joke.) When I was hired for the job, the younger guards would laugh at me behind my back. They would say I was too old to catch shoplifters. What they were not aware of was the fact that I had been shoplifting before they were born. I caught more shoplifters than any guards in the store. The shoplifters thought I was just some old person shopping. For instance, one day while I was on duty a shoplifter was watching me and I was watching her. She thought I was shoplifting because I had a large purse on my arm. I think she felt sorry for me because she walked up to me and said, "You are going to get caught." I said, "Oh yeah?" She said,

"You are looking around too much and you are too slow. Let me show you how it is done." I did not respond, I just watched her. She proceeded to show me how to shoplift without getting caught. When she had finished her shopping (shoplifting) we walked out of the store together. Once we were out of the store, I pulled out my badge and said, "Excuse me, I believe you left the store without paying for your merchandise." She grabbed her chest. I thought she was going to have a heart attack. She said, "I cannot believe you! You looked like a shoplifter."

After that incident I stopped stealing; not because I wanted to, but because I began to get careless. I did not want to go to jail. I had no remorse about what I was doing. I knew the difference between right and wrong, but doing wrong felt better than doing right. When I was a child I was told I would never amount to anything. Stealing was my way of proving that I could be good at something. It was a bad choice, but it was a choice that I will have to live with for the rest of my life. I know God has forgiven me, but I have not completely forgiven myself. Writing this book is my way of healing and hoping some-one who reads it will make a different choice. If you are a thief, stop before you get caught. Pray and ask God to deliver you from your stealing habit. I don't remember asking God to deliver me from stealing; however, somewhere along the line I lost the desire. When the devil tries to tempt me, I do as Jesus did. I tell him, "It is written, thou shall not steal." The Ten Commandments make it very clear that we are not to take anything that does not belong to us. If we don't acquire what we need through lawful means, we are stealing. The satisfaction I receive from not stealing is much greater than the satisfaction I received from stealing. When I stole there was the immediate gratification I felt from getting away with what I did, but I was never at peace with just getting away, I always had to have more. The satisfaction I get now is the peace and joy of the Lord, knowing that I have more than enough of everything I need.

Writing about this part of my life is the hardest thing I have had to do. Stealing, to me, is one of the worst things I have ever done. Writing about this has made me aware of what God means when he says he hates sin. All of the things I proudly did before, I now hate. I am not proud of what I did, but God wants me to show people what he can do with a thief or anyone else who sins. Romans 2:11: "For there is not respecter of persons with God." When you are a thief, you are a bond servant. The only way to be released from Satan's hold is through the blood of

Jesus. Jesus is also the only way you can remain free. Satan will never set you free. He will remind you, every chance he gets, of what a terrible person you are and he will tempt you every chance he gets. The important thing to remember is that you are no longer his servant if you are a child of God. You did not have a price to pay for your sins, but once that price is paid, it is finished.

Remember what Jesus said on the cross when he paid the price for our sins? He said, "It is finished." The same law applies to us today. When the price is paid, it is finished in the eyes of God. Hebrews 8:12: "For I will be merciful to their unrighteousness and their sins and their iniquities will I remember no more."

Satan is not qualified to forgive; therefore, in his eyes our sins are never forgiven. Unlike Satan, I am qualified to forgive. I must forgive my brother, who lied to me about why it was necessary to steal. My brother told me the white man had promised us (our grandparents, their slaves) a mule and forty acres of land. He said that by now the mule has died, but, he asked, where was the land? I told him I didn't know. He then said that we must steal to get whatever we feel the land would be worth today. I was foolish to ever believe him. I should have known better but I didn't.

I learned everything in my life the hard way because I did not seek God's advice. I would have been a lot better off if I had someone around to tell me about Jesus and about how much he loved me, no matter what I had done. I know now that God always pointed me the right way, but, in my mind, the wrong way was the easiest way. In my first drafts of this book I explained how I was trained by my brother, but after several drafts God laid it on my heart not to teach people how to steal, so I cannot tell about all the things I did to get what I needed, the easy way. What I must try to get people to understand is that the penalty for stealing is death (separation from God).

Chapter 9
BE ALL YOU CAN BE

I was sick and tired of packing tomatoes. I needed to find another job. As I was looking through Jet magazine I saw an ad that said, "Be all you can be." Next to the ad was a beautiful black woman wearing an army uniform. I said to myself, I want to look just like her. I quickly filled out the form attached to the ad. About two weeks later I received a call from a recruiter who said she would like to come by and talk with me. A few days later, there at my door stood a beautiful black woman. She looked just like the woman in the ad. I knew as soon as I saw her that I wanted to be like her. She asked me if I would like to see what an army base looked like. I said yes. I can't ever remember being so excited.

She took me to Fort Dix. When we drove on the post I thought I had died and gone to heaven. It was getting close to 5:00 when we finished looking around. I thought we were getting ready to leave, but instead she asked me if I would like to see the Non-Commissioned Officer's Club. I said yes, so after talking for a few minutes we decided to get something to drink. I ordered a rum and coke, but when the bartender returned he gave me two rum and cokes. I said, "I only ordered one drink." He said, "Five o'clock is happy hour, so you get two drinks for the price of one." I said what! So, I asked him, "If I order two drinks I will get four?" He said, "That's right." I said, "Make me happy and give me two drinks."

My decision was made. I had found heaven on earth. I joined the army because of happy hour. I had discovered a way to get double the alcohol for my money. They called it happy hour, but there are no happy hours once you become an alcoholic. The buy-one-and-get-one-free was a trick of the devil. No good can come from anyone who gives you something free that can and will destroy your health. It took the military a long time to realize they were destroying people's lives by contributing to the many other problems we had. As for myself, I paid a high price for those free drinks. For 20 years I drank alcohol. Only by the grace of God did I not destroy every organ in my body.

The army was my proving ground. I had the opportunity to prove how well I had been trained by my mother, cousin, and brother. In the military I entered my own private war. I went into the army to have fun and get drunk. I did not go in to listen to a white woman call me a nigger. My first assignment was to whip the first white girl who called me a nigger. After I did what I felt was necessary I went AWOL because I knew I was capable of murdering her, so it was best for me to leave. I left Alabama and I went to Atlanta. I called my recruiter and I told her what happened. She explained to me if they caught me that I would go to jail. She told me to go back and maybe they would let me out. I did not want to go to jail, so I took my chances and I went back.

The major I spoke with told me I had made a commitment to my country and it was my duty as a citizen to keep it. She said, "You can leave and let your country down or you can stand and honor your three-year commitment." I made the decision to stay, hoping that no white person got in my way or ever called me a nigger again. My dream of white people staying out of my way ended at my first duty station. A white major (military policeman) patted me on my rear as I passed by him. I slapped his face so hard he fell against the wall. He tried to press charges against me by stating that I had cursed him when he was correcting me. I went to the race relations office and told my side of the story to the officer in charge.

After I completed my story, the major called the officer and the charges were dropped. It appeared that this officer had a problem with his hands. He had used them before but no one did anything about it. The major was transferred from the Military Police organization. I was given a job working in the race relations office. I was given a stack of army regulations to read. The major who hired me told me to learn them by heart. He said, "If you expect to stay in the army you will have to know every regulation that pertains to you." He sent me to race relations Equal Opportunity School.

After I completed the six-week course, I taught classes and learned everything I could. For the next 19 years I was a walking regulation. I knew more about the regulations than most of my commanders. I established myself everywhere I went. I was an Equal Opportunity Representative, a legal clerk, a Drug and Alcohol Representative, and a Non Commissioned Officer Leaderships course instructor. If you noticed, two of the things I was responsible for while in the army were drugs and alcohol. This was not a job I selected or wanted because I was a heavy drinker at the time this job was forced on me. It all started when we got a new sergeant major in the battalion. I was working in the battalion as the legal clerk. I was a functioning alcoholic. I did my job and I did it well. I really did not want to be a part of that assignment because I was responsible for all the legal documentation for a battalion of over 800 people. Drunks and hangovers were common in the battalion; everyone looked out for one another. When I was too drunk or if I had a hangover I would place a hat on my desk with a purse. This would indicate that I was somewhere in the area, but in real life I would be in my room asleep. I would sleep until the hangover was gone.

After all, the only thing that was important was getting the work done on time. I was never late getting or completing a job and didn't even have to rush. I was good at my job. About two weeks after the new sergeant major took over, he called me into his office. He said, "Sergeant Knight, I have decided to put you in charge of Drug and Alcohol." I almost fainted. Who was this nut? I knew he could see the fear on my face. But I was cool; he just caught me off guard for a few minutes. I told him I didn't want that job. He said, "Do you know the difference in wanting something and not wanting something?" I said, "Sure, you either want it or you don't want it." He said, "I want you to take charge of Drug and Alcohol because I am the sergeant major. You don't want to take charge of it, but you have no choice in the matter. You are just a sergeant. Now answer me this question, which one of us gets what they want?" After that I said, "When do you want me to start?"

I took great pleasure in controlling and intimidating people around me, but I was not stupid. I could not intimidate this man. I knew I had to do what he said. After I started to work in Drug and Alcohol, I was ashamed for the soldiers to see me drunk. Little by little I stopped drinking during the week. I would only drink on Friday night and Saturday. I had to be focused for the job I was doing. My primary job function was testing urine for drugs. I was proud of myself because people feared me. I was in charge of several people, mostly men. When they would come to my office with samples that were not correct I would unleash the wrath of Josephine on them. I made men cry because of their poor performance. The procedure for testing and collecting urine had to be exact; there could be no mistakes. A mistake could get a soldier discharged from the service. I did not and would not be responsible for anyone being discharged.

I now find it amazing how my sense of right and wrong dictated my life. I did not think it was wrong to control and intimidate people. However, I felt it was wrong for a person to perform poorly in their job. The power, control, and sense of intimidation that I acquired when I was a child carried me through 20 years in the military. The abuse that was forced upon me as a child carried over to my adult life.

My greatest joy for the 20 years I was in the military was knowing that most of the people I dealt with were afraid of me. I used my job and my position to control people. My last two years in the army were the worst years. The leaders in my battalion did everything they could to put me out, but I knew the regulations and I used them to my advantage. There was one sergeant major who hated me. He told one of the sergeants that I was cocky. One day after I had made him mad he called me in his office and said to me, "Sergeant Knight, if it is the last thing I do, I am going to put you out of the army. You are useless and the army doesn't need you." I told him he was being unfair and that he was allowing his personal feelings to get in the way of his judgment.

I was sick because I fell and hurt my back. It was not my fault that I could no longer do the job he wanted me to do. The army had allowed me to work in an office for 18 years; now that I was sick, he was trying to force me to do a job that would require me to climb trees and telephone poles. I told him what he was doing was very unfair. He lay back in his chair, put his arms behind his head, and said, "That's life." I remember saying to myself, "Yep, you are right, it's your life." I walked out of his office, went to the rod and gun club, and picked out a .38 caliber pistol. I was surprised to learn how easy it was to get a gun. They gave me the paperwork, which needed to be signed by my commander. It is so amazing because he didn't even ask me why I wanted the gun, he just signed the papers. I went back to his office to kill him, but he was not there.

I thank God to this day that the sergeant major had left for the day. I decided to kill him on Monday morning, but over the weekend I realized I had forgotten to purchase bullets for the gun. By Monday I had cooled down. Not wanting to go to work, I went to mental hygiene. They sent me to the mental ward in the hospital. After three days of rest, the doctor said I was not crazy. He said I had a problem taking orders from people. I knew I was going to catch hell when I went back to my unit, so I convinced the doctors to let me attend a stress reduction class for one week. I told them I was afraid and that I needed to learn how to control my temper. The truth of the matter was that I wasn't afraid at all. My purpose in doing this was to get documentation of my treatment in the event I decided to use the gun later.

Once I convinced the doctors to let me enroll in the stress management class I was back in control of my life. My next step was to ensure no one messed with me, so I conjured up an imaginary dog. This dog walked with me everywhere I went. People would ask me who was I talking to and I would tell them I was talking to my dog, Spot. They left me alone after my sergeant found out about the gun and the people in the platoon started coming to tell him about my imaginary dog.

When the war Desert Storm began, I was the first one they put on the plane. I was sent to fight in a war even though I was ill and could barely walk. But, God saw fit for me to get a job where I was living in a house with a swimming pool across the street. When the commanders found out I was working the general's switchboard and living like a queen, they were sick. They sent me to Saudi Arabia to die, but God had other plans for my life. God has always blessed me, but because of my sinful nature, I disregarded God as the source of my blessing. I counted it all up to luck. When I returned from Saudi Arabia, I filed charges against my commander and the sergeant major. The sergeant major retired and the commander was reassigned to a different unit. After I got rid of all the people who had tried to get rid of me, I was left alone and allowed to retire in peace.

Sidebar: About two months before being sent to Saudi Arabia, Josey had applied for a class that she needed to get promoted to the next rank. The sergeant major and the commander refused to sign the paperwork for her to go because she had been on a physical profile for a long time and had not taken a physical fitness test. They told her she was out of shape so she could not go to the class. It was obvious to everyone doing the investigation that if he knew she was too out of shape to attend a class, she was certainly not qualified to go fight a war. She wrote everyone from Saudi and told them what a wonderful time she was having over there. She told them she would take care of business once she returned. She knew that someone was going to pay the consequences for sending her there.

One of the greatest sorrows of my life is that I

did not use the 20 years living for God and leading people to Christ. I wasted 20 years of my life trying to outsmart those who were in charge of me. Romans 13:7: "Render therefore to all their dues: tribute to whom tribute is due; custom to whom custom; fear to whom fear; honor to whom honor." When I returned from Saudi, the greatest joy of my life was to see the sergeant major who put me in charge of Drug and Alcohol. A few days before he retired, he called me in his office. He said, "Sergeant Knight, you are a smart woman, but you waste time trying to be smart. The first week I was here I knew you were an alcoholic. Putting the hat and the pocket book on the desk is an old trick that alcoholics have used for years. When I gave you the job as the Drug and Alcohol NCO it was to see if you really were as smart as I had heard you were. You proved to me that you were smart because you stopped drinking in order to perform your job. Stop wasting your life trying to prove you are smart. You are what you are. You do not have to prove what you are. Prove to others that you are more than what they see." After the sergeant major left the battalion, I stopped drinking. When I did start back to drinking, it no longer filled the void that was in my life. Through the grace of God I stopped drinking totally.

Chapter 10
I GIVE UP

Soon after I left Daisy's house I started to plan my suicide. I called my girl friend Stella to tell her how I wanted to be buried. Stella, whom I have known for ten years, was not home, so I talked with her husband. I can't remember what he said to me, but I did forget about suicide for a couple of days. I finally spoke with Stella. But before I tell you about the suicide, let me tell you a little about Stella. Every time you call Stella she acts as if she hasn't seen or heard from you in years. She is always cheerful and has a beautiful smile. I hated her when I first met her. We worked together in the same office. Maybe hate is a strong word, but the devil convinced me she was a phony Christian. I did everything I could to make her mad. One Friday after work she said, "Have a nice weekend, Josey." I looked at her and said, "I hope it rains this weekend and you get wet." I never will forget what she said. She said, "That will be all right. I still love you." She didn't know it, but she was the first person who ever said they loved me and meant it. Her husband told me she said I was the meanest person she had ever met. She told him she was going to pray for me.

To my knowledge, she is the first person who ever prayed for me. Well, about ten years have passed and she is my best friend. She is still praying for me. Stella is the only person I know who can rebuke you with total grace and style. I have had several of her graceful rebukes over the years. I thank her for them because I know that she loves me and God has given her the wisdom and knowledge to put me back on the track whenever I slip off.

Now back to my suicide attempt. When I finally spoke to Stella I told her I could not take the pain and the loneliness anymore. I told her the devil had shown me an image of myself sitting in a wheelchair in a gray uniform. He (the devil) told me he had already killed my mother, my sisters, my brother, and the rest of my family. Now he was going to kill me. He told me I could end the pain and the lonely nights by killing myself. He told me to jump off the balcony and it would be all over. I was afraid to jump, but I was more afraid of living my life without hands and legs.

When I told her about everything that was happening she told me not to worry and that everything was going to be all right. I remember saying to myself, "How in the hell can she be so cheerful when I am getting ready to kill myself? Doesn't she know or care that I am getting ready to kill myself?" She told me to read the 91st Psalm. I told her I would but at that point I didn't want to hear anything about the Bible. After all, it was God's fault I was sick. He had put me here on this earth and left me here to fend for myself.

After we spoke I started to read the Psalm. I remember reading the fourth verse (Psalms 91:4). "He shall cover thee with his feathers and under his wings shall thou trust. His truth shall be thy shield and bucker." I said to myself, "Wow! What kind of bird is this? It must be a big bird to cover someone with his feather." This shows you how much I knew about the Bible. I thought they were talking about an actual big bird. As I continued to read, I became even more confused. I called Stella back and told her I didn't understand what I was reading. She told me to read the Psalm three times but to pray first and ask the Lord to give me understanding of what I was reading. I prayed and it was as if a light lit up and focused directly on the verses I was reading. God began to show me his powers. It was unbelievably amazing how well I understood what I read. When I spoke with her later on, she asked me if I had ever heard of T.D. Jakes. I told her I thought I had seen him once on television. She told me I needed to look at some of his tapes. She also said that someone was going to come into my life to help me and to mentor me. The next day as I was walking down the hall I saw someone who had been in the military with me. Her name was Joyce and she knew I was a hell raiser. As a matter of fact, she was the only person in my unit who knew the regulations better than I did. They tried to get her to do the paperwork to put me out of the army, but she refused to do it because she knew what they were trying to do was wrong.

When we were in the military I did not know Joyce was a Christian, but for some reason I never cursed her or had any trouble with her. Only God knew that she and I would get together later on in life. Joyce was a lot like Stella in many ways. As a matter of fact, I sometimes would call Stella Joyce and Joyce Stella. Joyce always had a smile on her face too. When I first met her I thought she was a little nutty. You know what I mean, one of those phony

Christians. When I would meet her in the hallway, we would always speak and have a small conversation. I asked her if she had ever heard of T.D. Jakes. She said yes and that she had almost all of his tapes. I asked her to bring some of them in so I could see them and she immediately said she would.

Sidebar: When I learned about Josey in Germany, it was from her platoon sergeant. He wanted me to help him put her out of the army. She had been in the army for 17 years working as a clerk or doing some type of office work that kept her from going to the field with her platoon. They let her get away with that and never required her to work in her MOS as a field wireman. This really was a man's job, but when the doors opened for women to join the military, this job was included as acceptable for women. The only time they could actually do this job was when we went out in the field to install communication lines. It consisted of them stumping through the woods laying wire and telephone lines throughout the camp we had set up and the adjacent camps. You had to climb trees to lift the lines across the road. The cable was heavy and you had to do this in all kinds of weather, hot, cold, rain, or snow. I would not have wished it on any woman or my worst enemy. She had less than three years left in the army before retiring and they wanted to take away her retirement. The army had allowed her to escape her duties thus far and I wasn't going to help them try to rectify a wrong that should have been corrected from the beginning.

The first tape I remember looking at was "Sacrifice of Praise." When the altar call was given at the end of the tape, I threw up my hands and repeated the sinner's prayer. I was saved. I know I was saved because of what happened the next day. I was driving along enjoying my day when suddenly, someone pulled out in front of me. I tried to curse, but the words would not come out. I used to curse all the time. The words would automatically come out of my mouth, but God took that right away. I can still curse, but I have no desire to do so.

The next thing I noticed was that I was no long afraid of lightning. When I was a child my cousin would make me sit in a corner during thunderstorms. She would tell me to be quiet while God was doing his work. She taught me to fear lightning. This fear carried over into my adult life. The second day after I was saved, there was a terrible storm. As I lay in bed I remembered thinking, something is strange. By this time the lightning was lighting up the room, but there was no fear. 2 Timothy 1:7: "For God hath not given us the spirit of fear, but of power, of love and of a sound mind."

Thus began my walk with Christ. I was saved, but the devil did not give up. He still tried to get me to jump off of the balcony. I remember one day he was tormenting me about my family and he said to me, "Jump!" I remember saying out loud, "Why don't you jump the hell off the balcony?" I balled up my fist and was ready to fight. Little did I know that the devil is not someone you can fight alone. I started watching religious tapes and reading about God. I knew I had it made now that I was a real Christian. I joined the first church I walked into. That was the wrong thing to do, but I will discuss that later.

God started to train me. My first experience of God's great love was during my second week of being a Christian. I was lying in bed when something (I say something because I didn't know what the Holy Spirit was at the time) told me to turn over. As I turned over there was a man standing in my bed.

His feet were not touching the bed. He had on a white robe with a sash around his waist. His hair was shoulder length. I did not see his face, but I clearly remember his staff. I remember how peaceful it was. I remember the 23rd Psalms: "For thou art with me, thy rod and thy staff they comfort me." I told everybody I knew about what I had seen. Mostly all of them looked at me like I was a nut except my friend Joyce. She would always say, "Enjoy it now while you are a babe in Christ because later it's going to get tougher." Luke 12:48: "But he that knew not, and did commit things worthy of stripes, shall be beaten with few stripes. For unto whomsoever much is given, of him shall be much required: and to whom men have committed much, of him they will ask the more." I figured she told me that because she was just jealous.

Sometime during that first month, God woke me up and told me to read the book of Peter. After I finish reading Peter, he told me to go to Isaiah. Now, I had heard about Peter, but I had never heard about Isaiah. So when God told me to go to Isaiah I said, "Go to his house?" He said, "Read." When I finished reading Isaiah he told me to read Deuteronomy; so, I started to read but it was too hard to understand. At this point it appeared God had stopped talking to me.

I was very upset because I was accustomed to God waking me up and telling me to read different scriptures. I got in the habit of taking my paper and pencil to bed with me. I asked Joyce why God didn't talk to me anymore. She said, "Because you did not follow his instructions. He told you to read and you didn't. Until you finish what he has instructed you to do, he might not talk." I told her it was too hard to read. The next thing she told me to do was to pray each time before I read. I prayed just like she told me. I read and I understood. I was very excited until I got to the place where he tells them to kill all the people and the animals. (You will have to read the sixth and seventh chapter of Joshua to understand what happened.)

Joshua 7:24-25: "Then Joshua, together with all Israel, took Achan son of Zerah, the silver, the robe, the gold wedge, his sons and daughters, his cattle, donkeys and sheep, his tent and all that he had, to the Valley of Achor. **25** Joshua said, 'Why have you brought this trouble on us? The LORD will bring trouble on you today.' Then all Israel stoned him, and after they had stoned the rest, they burned them." When I read this I was devastated. I thought, what kind of God is this that kills people? Candice, another Christian lady who had come into my life during my first month as a Christian, explained to me why

God did what he did.

Ephesians 5:6: "Let no one deceive you with empty words, for because of such things God's wrath comes on those who are disobedient." She explained what I did not understand.

Chapter 11
SALVATION AND DELIVERANCE

I could not take the pain and the loneliness any longer. I was tired of waking up every day sick. I just wanted to give up. The doctor had informed me that I had diabetes. My sister died from diabetes and I believed I was going to die from the same disease. The idea of being alone and handicapped was too much for me to handle. The few friends I had lived far away from me. I decided that death was better than living. I had not decided how I was going to end my life, but I felt I had no other choice.

I called Stella to go over the details of my funeral arrangements. Stella was not home, so I talked with her husband, Paul. Paul is not the type of person I would think about calling if I were planning to kill myself. He and I always joked with each other about everything but never anything as serious as this. On that particular day when I called I was not in a joking mood. It seemed that Paul has always been the person who was there to witness to me each time I thought my life was not worth living.

One thing I have learned in my quest for survival is that God makes the decision of who will minister for him. When I called I wanted Stella, but God used Paul instead. I didn't even know Paul was capable of witnessing to anyone. I cannot remember what he said, but whatever he said must have had some impact on me because I forgot all about ending my life for the moment. A few days later, I called again to find Stella at home. She said she had not returned my call because she was unable to find my number. She had placed my number in her Rolodex but was unable to find it. Two days after we spoke she called me back to let me know that my telephone number was in her Rolodex just like she said it was. She had wasted two days looking for it but could not find it.

Before I finished discussing my aches, pains and desire to end my life, Stella told me how much they loved me and had accepted me as one of the family. It really lifted my spirit and changed my mind because I knew she meant it. Stella told her husband that I was changing into a very nice person. I believe God placed Stella in my life to be my quardian angel here on earth.

Now that you know a little about Stella we can get back to my decision to end my life.

The more I read, the more confused I became. I called Stella back and I told her I didn't understand what I was reading. She told me to read the Psalm three times. She said, "I want you to pray and ask God to illuminate (to supply or brighten with light/ to make understandable) his word so that you will be able to understand." I knew what the word illuminate meant, but what I was trying to figure out was how God was going to light up the Bible. I had seen The Ten Commandments several times and I didn't want to have a Moses experience. I didn't want no Bible lighting up in my hands or my hair turning gray. I didn't have much knowledge of how God did things. There I was, a little concerned about how he was going to help me to understand. If I had not been so afraid and confused, I probably would not have touched the Bible, but at that moment I was willing to try anything. I prayed and asked God to illuminate the Bible so that I might understand what I read. If God could make me understand and if I could experience the happiness that Stella always displayed, I wanted him to do so.

As I began to read, it seemed as if the words stood

out on the page. I understood everything I read. I had never experienced anything like it. It was one of the happiest days of my life. I could not believe how well I understood. It is now several years later and the 91st Psalm is still my favorite Psalm. Whenever I witness to others, I always tell them to make the 91st Psalm a part of their study and their life. When I was studying the 91st Psalm I realized that everything I needed and everything I desired was in accepting Jesus as my refuge. Verses 1-8 taught me about the safety I have with God when I make him my refuge. Verses 9-16 showed me his favor and his protection over my life. Notice that for this Psalm, Christ provides a personal glimpse into his heart with each verse. Making God a part of my life would provide me with all of his promises. Now the question was how could I get these promises.

As in any biblical study, we must seek to understand what we are studying in order to apply what we learn to our life. To help me understand the 91st Psalm I designed a diagram. Whenever I feel like I do not have anyone to love me or anyone to lean on in times of trouble, I look at my diagram and it reminds me that I have a secret place to go where I can be delivered from any problems or pain. I don't have to worry about anyone or anything because God is my refuge. No harm will or can come near me because he gives his angels charge over me. I have seen one of my angels and even I would not mess with them. The one I saw was over six feet and very, very big.

Some things we do are automatic, such as blinking our eyes and breathing. These things are normal bodily functions. Cursing is a weapon used by Satan. According to Webster's II dictionary, cursing is used to invoke evil, calamity, or injury. Because no good can be gained by cursing, God showed me I did not have to curse. I no longer needed to invoke evil, calamity (misery), or injury toward people. It is God's desire that we use our mouth to preach the gospel. When we use our mouth to curse we are letting the devil use what is meant for God.

When I became a Christian I know I made the Devil mad. He and I had been together for many years. He did not intend to let me go without a fight. But God prepared me by giving me the tools and the people I needed to do battle. These tools can be found in Ephesians 6:10-17. "Finally, my brethren, be strong in the Lord, and in the power of his might. Put on the whole armor of God that ye may be able to stand against the wiles of the devil. For we wrestle not against flesh and blood, but against principalities, against powers, against the rulers of the darkness of this world, against spiritual wickedness in high places. Wherefore take unto you the whole armor of God that ye may be able to withstand in the evil day, and having done all to stand, stand therefore, having your loins girt about with truth, and having on the breastplate of righteousness; and your feet shod with the preparation of the gospel of peace; above all, taking the shield of faith, wherewith ye shall be able to quench all the fiery darts of the wicked. Take the helmet of salvation and the sword of the Spirit, which is the word of God." (KJV)

God surrounded me with women who are strong in the faith. The reason I say these women are strong is because God told me they were and why they were in my life. God showed me that when I became a Christian I still retained parts of my personality. God and only God knew I was going to need more than one person to keep me on track. God also knew that if the person had been weak in their faith I would chew them up and spit them out. I thank God for each of the women because each one of them has been and still is a part of my spiritual life.

Chapter 12
NEW LIFE

Here I was, a new Christian who had just watched at least ten of T.D. Jakes' tapes, in a traditional Baptist church and ready to praise the Lord. Something was very wrong with this picture. There was only one lady present who had nerve enough to raise her hands up. The songs they sang were "Amazing Grace" and "How I Got Over." Well, I figured they just had to warm up. But what I later discovered was exactly what I saw the first Sunday I attended, and that was about as warm as their service was going to get. I joined that church the first Sunday I attended. The church was a quiet church and the people were like family. That was the biggest mistake I could have ever made.

As time went by I found out they believed God only healed in the old treatment. The more I went to the church the more I felt like I was missing something. I told Joyce that I felt like I was going to a store the day before a holiday. There is very little left on the shelf. Joyce told me if I started to speak in tongues they were going to put me out of the church. On the following Sunday I prayed a little too loud. The person sitting next to me jumped like I had touched her with a hot coal. I want you to know I didn't do that anymore.

A few weeks after I had joined the church God spoke to me in a dream. He said, "I want you to be just like Paul." Now, I did not know who Paul was, so I asked the pastor. He asked me why I had asked that question. I told him God told me to be like Paul. He told me who Paul was, but he also said something that made me feel like he thought I was not being truthful. After this incident I was very careful of whom I talked to about God talking to me. I thought God talked to all Christians. Some Christians told me that they had never heard him speak to them. I did not understand this. I knew I was not making up the things I said. I didn't even know who Paul was. I began to feel that some of the people I told about God speaking to me were jealous. After a while I stopped telling people what God was teaching me.

As I look back over my life I can remember God was always talking to me and giving me instructions, but I chose not to follow those instructions.

I King 19:

[11]And he said, Go forth, and stand upon the mount before the LORD. And, behold, the LORD passed by, and a great and strong wind rent the mountains, and brake in pieces the rocks before the LORD; but the LORD was not in the wind: and after the wind an earthquake; but the LORD was not in the earthquake.

[12]And after the earthquake a fire; but the LORD was not in the fire: and after the fire a still small voice.

[13]And it was so, when Elijah heard it, that he wrapped his face in his mantle, and went out, and stood in the entering in of the cave. And, behold, there came a voice unto him, and said, what doest thou here, Elijah?

Now that I think about it, I was never alone. God was with me all the time. If I had known about him, I know my life would be totally different than what it is now. In him I had a father, mother, and friend that I could turn to anytime I needed him. He was there all the time and all I had to do was to reach out and touch him, but I didn't know it.

Chapter 13
GETTING TO KNOW CANDICE

The next experience in my Christian walk was getting to know Candice. Candice was in the deliverance ministry. I met her through Joyce. There was something about her that got on my nerves. At times I hated her, and at other times I just didn't want to be around her. She told me that I had some demons in me and I needed to be delivered from them. I thought, *This woman is sick and trying to look important.* She asked me if she could come to my house and pray with me. I told her she could, knowing all along I was not going to let her in. I knew she was a witch or, at the least, in a cult. I would lie to her and sometimes I would even hide from her. This kept up for about a month. The devil told me to stay away from her. I would get sick to my stomach sometimes when I talked to her. Somehow, I can't remember how, she convinced me to let her come to my house. I only allowed her to come because I trusted Joyce. The night she came, Joyce came with her. It was around seven o'clock when they arrived. From seven that night to three o'clock in the morning, we wrestled with many demonic spirits. I will never forget that night because I got delivered from a lot of demonic spirits. Candice was praying in the spirit and getting instructions from the Holy Spirit while Joyce prayed and read the Bible. We went from the couch to the floor to the chair over and over again. Some of the demonic spirits talked to me and begged me not to make them leave. You see, they have a legal right to stay if you want them to stay. I can truly say, that night "we overcame the devil by the blood of the lamb and the words of our testimony; and they loved not their lives unto the death." (Revelation 12:11)

If anyone had told me there would be demons in a person I would have called them a fruitcake. (Matthew 17:21) "However, this kind does not go out except by prayer and fasting." The devil knew I was capable of fooling people and getting my way because he taught me how to do this for years. Like many of you who are reading this book, you do not believe what you are reading. You do not believe in demonic spirits. I didn't believe in them either until that night. I can't remember all of the demons, but I can tell you about those that I do remember.

There was one that begged Candice not to make him leave. He said he had always been with me and he did not want to leave. He told her he had no place to go. I lay in Candice's arms because she reminded me of my mother. I tried to trick her by telling her that I loved her. Nevertheless, she was good and she knew I was lying. I believed there were seven or eight demonic spirits in me. Joyce was travailing in the spirit on the floor. Revelation 12:2: "And she, being with child, cried travailing in birth, and pained to be delivered." I tried to let go of the demon that appeared to be controlling me because I could see that Joyce was in pain. No matter what they said or did, he was not letting go. He was smart, controlling, and condescending. He knew everything about me because he had been with me when my mother and my father were not there. He was not about to let go that easy. He told me, "She (Candice) looks like your mother. She doesn't love you. She's a phony. You don't have any demons in you. This is just the way you are. Why are you worrying about demons; you are saved. So fake it by pretending you are throwing up so she will believe I am gone."

I did just what he said. However, I didn't fool

Joyce or Candice. They knew I was faking. After about seven hours it was over for the night. When Candice left she told me to read the Bible and pray for the gift of speaking in tongue. I thought, I am glad to know that she is finally leaving. I learned later that when you cast out the devil you must fill that empty space with the spirit of the Holy Ghost. Matthew 12:43-44: "When the unclean spirit is gone out of a man, he walketh through dry places, seeking rest, and findeth none. Then he saith, I will return into my house from whence I came out; and when he is come he findeth it empty, swept and garnished." You must fill that empty space with the Holy Spirit so that the evil spirits cannot return.

Sidebar: Candice and I left Josey's apartment at 2:00 a.m. that morning. I was so tired when I got home all I wanted to do was go to sleep. When I walked in the door my husband came running down the steps in his underwear wanting to know where I had been all this time. He had a legitimate reason for being upset because this had never happened before. I should have called home to let him know where I was, but I was so preoccupied with what I was doing, I totally forgot. I was completely drained of energy and I did not want to be bothered with his questions at that moment. I went straight upstairs and went to bed. If he wanted to argue he would have to do it by himself because I was out like a light as soon as my head hit the pillow.

Candice and I had worked so hard with Josey. We had prayer teams in Georgia and Colorado praying and interceding for us as we dealt with Josey. We knew we had not cast the strongman out, which was anger/rage. Other spirits we found in Josey that we could identify were hatred, strife, revenge, spite, cruelty, envy, jealousy, and lying. We knew it was not over and that we would have to go back again. She seemed to hold on to her strongman because he had been with her since she was a little girl. You can do everything you can to cast out a demon, but if the person does not want to be rid of it, it has a right to stay with that person. Once that person denounces that spirit, it is easy to get rid of it. I called Candice and told her we could meet at Josey's church and go with her home from there.

Josey called me on Saturday and said

she had received the gift of the speaking in tongues. I believed it to be a trick from the enemy, but I didn't tell her that. She was happy to give me a demonstration of her tongues over the phone. I listened but did not say a word. I told her we would meet her at her church on Sunday and she said okay. I received a call from Sister Hicks, who led the prayer chain in Colorado. She said she had received a word from the Lord about Josey. The word was, "It will not take long this time; the foundation has been laid." I was excited to hear that because I thought it would be another long, drawn-out episode of delivering Josey from her strongman.

Candice and I arrived at the church at 11:00 sharp. She was waiting for us inside the foyer area of the church. We had her sit in the middle of us so we could observe her actions. During the service I glanced into Josey's eyes and saw the enemy, who had put a smug, leery grin on her face and just like that it disappeared. I knew it was not over. When church let out we told Josey we were going to meet her at her house. She said okay but she needed to go get some water from the grocery store. I said okay, we would wait for her. Candice followed me to Josey's house and we waited for her in my car. It didn't seem like it because we were talking, but an hour later Josey finally drove up. She could not see our cars so I guess she thought we had got tired of waiting and left. She strutted out of the car and up the sidewalk with nothing in her hand but her purse. It was obvious she had not gotten any water. We got out of the car and walked to the elevator where we found Josey. She didn't even try to explain why she was empty-handed but was very shocked to see us. We went in and continued from where we had left off on Friday night. In two hours we were finished and Josey was filled with the Holy Ghost with the evidence of speaking in tongues.

I wanted to speak in tongues so bad. I prayed and I cried until God gave it to me. I did not realize that you do not have to beg God for a gift that he freely gives. Luke 11:13: "If you then, though you are evil, know how to give good gifts to your children, how much more will your Father in heaven give the Holy Spirit to those who ask him!" Candice did not believe me when I told her God had given me the gift. But I knew what had happened. I was sitting on my bed singing a song and all of a sudden I started to speak in a language that was unknown to me. I allowed Candice to test me and she said it was the spirit of God. Several months later Candice died. Candice's last words to me were, "Josephine, you be careful, don't let the devil trick you. He wants you back, be careful."

For the first time in my entire life I felt like I was free. Off and running, I ran to the closest church I could find, which was four blocks away from my house and was a traditional Baptist church. None of the traditional Baptist churches practice the gifts of healing and speaking in tongues. Now, I didn't know that you couldn't speak in tongues while you were in church. I didn't know that you could not praise the Lord with your hands raised high in worship or speak out in a loud voice.

The next thing that occurred to me was that I dreamed I was in heaven and there was a big choir there singing. They had on blue and white robes in the dream. I asked someone where I was. They said, "You are in heaven." I believed God was talking to me so I jumped up and ran to the altar. That made the devil mad.

Chapter 14
THE WORD, THE PASTOR, AND THE CHURCH

A few weeks later Joyce invited me to her church (Jericho Baptist church, now called Jericho City of Praise). As soon as I sat down I realized the choir I saw in heaven in my dream was the choir I saw in this church. The seating arrangement was exactly what I had seen in my dream. On the Sundays I went to Jericho I felt like I had been to church. I loved the way the pastor preached. She made sure you understood everything she said by repeating all the important points at least twice. I kept this up for about a month. Now, as I have stated many times in this story, I am not afraid of anything or anyone, but I am afraid of God.

During the time I was going to Jericho I always sat in the back because we were always late getting to church. One particular Sunday we were directed to come to the front of the church. We were given a seat in the center aisle three rows from the front. After the pastor finished preaching she had altar call. During altar call she said, "Some of you here know you are in the wrong church. You know you are supposed to be here in a church that teaches and preaches the word of God. God has led you here, so get up out of your seat and come on up here to this altar." At that point it appeared like she was pointing right at me. I felt in my spirit she was talking to me, so I jumped up and ran to the altar. The day I joined Jericho was the happiest day of my life. I didn't know that I was making the devil mad. I felt better about life than I had ever felt before.

At Jericho I began to grow in the word of the Lord. My friends were amazed at how fast I was changing. Not only was I being taught the word in the church, but God would wake me up between 2:30 and 3:00 every other morning to give me something to read. When I first became a Christian I could not wait to get home from work to read the Bible. I was so excited to know that God loved me. I would get very excited when the pastor would tell us how much God loved us. She had a way of making you feel that you are what God says you are. The one thing I enjoyed about her teaching was that she always showed you what she said was from the word of God.

After about a year or so of her teaching and preaching, I began to get bored. I felt like I knew everything there was to know. I began to get self-righteous. I felt like I had outgrown Jericho and I needed to find another church. At some point I began to tune the pastor out. I began to notice things that I had not noticed before. For example, she said "glory to God" after every sentence. I could not figure out why she did that. Then there was the praise and worship that lasted two to three hours. I felt it didn't take all of that to get to God. Little by little I started to stay away from church. The thing that finally pulled me away was when the Jubilee Celebration started. The excitement of the members was too much for me. Another thing I did not like was that there were too many children in the church and for some reason they always sat by me. No matter where I went to sit, there was always a baby. I said, "Enough is enough," and I left the church.

I stayed away from the church for several months. I missed the pastor and her teaching. Every time I would make up my mind to go back I would get sick or I had something else to do. Sunday was the only day I had to take care of personal things. I justified not going to church by watching the gospel programs on TV. After all, preaching was preaching. I would stay up until two o'clock Monday morning just to make sure God would forgive me for not going to church. In my mind, as long as I was doing something, he would not mind if I didn't go to church. As hard as I tried I could not stay away from Jericho.

One Saturday night I decided it was time for me to go back to church. I dreamed I was getting ready to go to church but I was late. When I got to the door the devil was standing there waiting for me. I don't know how I knew this was the devil because this man looked just like someone who worked in the building with me who is not saved. I knew this was the devil. In the dream I remembered what the pastor had told us about using the name of Jesus to make the devil flee. When I said, "Jesus, Jesus, Jesus," the man who appeared to be the devil backed away, but he did not go far. He stood in my yard by a car at this time and started to mock me. He said, "Jesus, Jesus, Jesus." When he did this he had his hands on his hips, mocking me like little kids do. I woke up and my spirit said, "You see, you don't have any power." God's spirit said to me, "Your power and your covenant are in the church. If you are not covered by the church the devil will control you." I wasted no time going back to church, but after a few weeks I left again. There was just too much noise for me. I felt I could be covered in any church; it didn't have to be Jericho.

I quickly found out I was wrong. I began to get sick and the devil started to take control of my thoughts. All of the things I did before I became a Christian came back to haunt me. I almost lost one of my best friends during this time. The desire to drink alcohol came back, but I did not drink. I was depressed most of the time. Now that I had left the church, my life was falling apart. I knew I was wrong for leaving, but I knew God was still God, so I prayed for him to show me a way to make things work.

Chapter 15
MY BUSINESS VENTURE

Joyce and I had started a business together. She used her money to start the business because I didn't have any to contribute. Little by little I began to hate being around her. I felt that she thought she was better than I was because she had money. I felt like she was trying to control me and the business. I had no intention of letting her have any control over me. I knew the devil was trying to break up our friendship. I was the one who found the shop. I was the one who took her to the places to open the shop. I was the one who got the people to rent space in the shop. I did everything I could to make the shop look good. So what if it was her money. I was convincing myself that she was using me for her advancement.

I felt like the devil was trying to break up our relationship, but I didn't know how to stop him. I didn't want to lose one of the only friends I had ever had. Every time I saw her I wanted to curse her out, but I knew if I cursed her she would not be my friend anymore. Keeping Joyce as my friend was more important to me than being in business with her. I waited for God's answer to my prayers. I decided to tell her that I no longer wanted to be a part of the business. On the day I had made up my mind to tell her, I was still undecided about what to say to her. When I got in my car that morning I turned on my radio to WYCB, "Heaven 1580." The announcer said, "The question of the day is 'Why Christians should let things of the world break up their friendship." I knew that this was my answer. I was allowing something of the world to destroy our friendship. I knew this was God's answer to me and I had made the right decision. When I told Joyce I was leaving she asked me how I was doing. At first I did not understand what she meant, but then she said, "I am not concerned about the bills, but I am wondering about you." She had to pay all of the bills by herself after I left, but her main concern was about my spiritual stability. She had known me for about ten years. She knew me when I was a sinner and she was there with me when those demons were cast out of my body. She was very concerned about me not coming to church. She was concerned that

I would return to the way I was before I became a Christian.

Matthew 12:44-45: "Then it says, 'I will return to the house I left.' When it arrives, it finds the house unoccupied, swept clean and put in order. [45]Then it goes and takes with it seven other spirits more wicked than itself, and they go in and live there. And the final condition of that man is worse than the first. That is how it will be with this wicked generation."

As I left the shop she walked with me to the van. She didn't know how much it hurt me to leave the store because this was my dream, but her friendship meant too much to me to stay. When I got to the van she hugged me and said, "Josephine, I love you. I really love you and I don't want anything to come between our friendship." She will never know how much that meant to me. Her love, encouragement, financial support, and cheerful smile have pulled me through many days. I thank God for placing Joyce in my life. I don't always understand how God uses people, but I know on many occasions after I have witnessed to a person, I will become ill and pains will come in my stomach. When this happens, although I have other friends, God will instruct me to call Joyce. When I call Joyce and we talk, the conversation always ends with me laughing and without pain. Joyce never fails to remind me that the devil hates me and any Christian who witnesses for God.

Sidebar: Both Josey and I worked at Bailey Cross Roads, which was right off of Columbia Pike. One day she called me and told me she wanted me to see this place because she knew I had been looking for an inexpensive place to open a gift shop. My hobby of ceramics had turned my house into a "store with plenty of products but no sales." I needed an outlet to sell these products. I told her I would meet her at lunchtime and I did. It was a portion of a bookstore that was not being used. I was selling my ceramics through a customer base I had accumulated by volunteering at the craft shop wherever I was stationed. I was also doing shows and open markets. I really had not planned to get a shop so soon, but I had talked with Josey about it several times. I was thinking maybe in a couple of years I would have gathered other craftsmen to join me to open a shop. Well, she called me all excited about this place that was for rent and that we could go in together to get it. She told me if we got it now, she would get other people to rent spaces from us to curtail the rental cost. I agreed to do this because I knew she did not have the money to get it on her own. She was doing baskets to sell and I must say they were beautiful. Our shop was surrounded by glass except for the back wall. That was advertisement in itself, but she was not satisfied with that. She took out ads that she could not afford. She also made the baskets more expensive than she was selling them for. When I tried to explain this to her, she got upset. I know she thought I was jealous of her baskets but I wasn't. This was in August. I was supposed to start college in September so I quit my job. We decorated and stocked the shelves right away. Business was going slow, but that was expected since we had just started with no advertising. It did pick up a little for me, but Josey's baskets weren't selling fast at all. I didn't realize it at the time, but it seemed that everything I suggested doing, she would oppose it. At some point I did recognize her negativity toward me. I quickly learned not to argue with her. She would come in every evening to check her merchandise to see if she had made any sales. I did not know it at the time, but she had put an ad out about her basket business. Had I known about it, we could have gone in together with the ad. She was competing against me, but I wasn't in the competition. After the second month she did not have money to pay half of the rent, but I told her it was okay. She could just rent a space from me for her baskets for a small fee. As a matter of fact, after that I opened the shop up to other crafters who needed an outlet to house their crafts and sell them. This setup provided me money to pay the rent and to help other crafters at the same time. When Josey would run out of money and wasn't able to pay her portion of the rental space as we had agreed upon, she would get angry. I could tell how easy it was for me to upset her. It seemed like she was angry at me all the time, but I overlooked it because I know how the enemy can slip in and cause problems and confusion. I just continued to pray for her and ask the Lord to help me stay calm. I know that the enemy had cut her off from people before and had used her anger to isolate her from everyone so that he could destroy her. I also knew that she did not have any family or friends here. It was no surprise to me the day Josey came to tell me she was not going to be in business with me anymore. I had already seen the signs and knew it would be just a matter of time. I could feel her animosity toward me. I knew she resented me for having a little money saved so that I could take on this venture. She was like a sister to me and I only wanted to help her. After she left the shop we got along well because she was focusing on her book.

Chapter 16
SUPERNATURAL POWERS

When I woke up I realized it was late and I had less than 20 minutes to get dressed. It was 8:15 now and I had to leave my house no later than 8:35 to get to work on time. When I finally left at 8:45, the first thing I noticed was that there were no cars on the street. I lived on one of the main streets running through the city. I asked myself, "Is today Sunday?" The drive from my house to work is approximately four miles. During the drive I saw no cars on the left or right of the street. What I did see was a tall, skinny white man step out onto a four-lane highway not looking left or right. I kept saying to myself, "He will look and stop," but he continued to walk, and before I knew it he was in front of my car. I slammed on the brakes and the man continued to walk across the street without even looking back at me or the van. I remembered saying that he must have a death wish. I looked back through my rearview mirror to see him standing on the side of the street looking in the direction of my van. I was a little shook up, but it passed quickly. When I pulled into the parking lot I noticed one of the ladies I worked with standing outside. I asked her what was she doing and she said, "I am waiting to see the baby." One of the people who worked with us was bringing her newborn baby by the office so everyone could see it. When she finally arrived she was surprised to see me at work before 9:00 a.m. When her husband got out of the car God laid it on my heart to ask him if he was a Christian. I pulled him aside and asked if he was a Christian. His answer was no. We spoke for a few minute and I led him through the sinner's prayer.

By the time I got to my desk I was in severe pain. My feet and legs were hurting so bad I could barely walk. I called Joyce but the pain was so bad I had to hang up in the middle of the conversation. A few minutes after we spoke, the pain stopped. I called Joyce back to tell her about the man walking in front of my car. She asked me if I knew what a divine appointment was. I said no. She said a divine appointment is when God has something for you to do and no devil in hell can stop you. I don't know what or who that was who walked in front of my car, but I do know he did not look at me or my car even though I was less than two feet from him. I also know that the street I travel on every day always has plenty of traffic except on Sunday morning. If I had hit whatever walked in front of my van, I would not have been in the parking lot that morning at the time God planned for me to be there to be a witness for him.

After the encounter with the man walking in front of my van, I knew I needed to go back to church, but my pride would not let me go back. What I did not realize was that Satan was calling the shots. I was looking for another church because Satan knew I was being taught the word of God at Jericho. I had begun to believe that I could think and plan my life independently of what God said. He had led me to Jericho and every time I left he led me right back. I finally realized that Satan was trying to render me powerless. He was doing it through a spirit of pride. Prov. 23.7: "For as a man thinks in his heart, so is he." (NKJV) I was allowing Satan to destroy all that I had gained through studying God's word.

If I fail to get you to understand or believe anything else you read in the Bible, know this: You cannot be covered in just any church. The church that God places you in is the one where your covering is.

Satan will use everything he can to get you to leave the place where you are protected. As long as you are in the church that God placed you in, Satan cannot touch you. All he can do is project thoughts to your mind. If you sit under a pastor who knows the words, you are protected. After going through all I have been through because of disobedience, I now realize why the pastor says God words repeatedly and that is so they will sink into your memory. If we do not get it the first time because we are not paying attention, we will get it the second, third, or in some cases the fourth time. I thank God for my pastor. She is the fourth strong spirit-led woman God has placed in my life.

On December 13, 1998, I went back to church. When I walked in the door the pastor said, "The message today is about familiar spirits." I knew I was supposed to be there. The pastor said, "Familiar spirits know everything about us. We invite them in and set up a table and feed them." When she said this I got a sickening feeling in the bottom of my stomach because I remembered what Joyce had told me about unclean (familiar spirits). My experience with familiar spirits was one that I will never forget. I stopped drinking alcohol before I became a Christian. This was one of those things that I never asked God to help me with; he just did it. Approximately two months after I became a Christian, I had a strong, uncontrollable desire to drink. I drank two cans of beer and it made me drunk. I knew something was not right about this because before when I was drinking, I could drink a pint of hard liquor and not get drunk. When I became drunk from the beer, I felt as if the devil had won. I believed God would not forgive me. I called Joyce and the conversation went something like this:

Josey: Joyce, guess what? He won.

Joyce: Who won?

Josey: The devil.

Joyce: What do you mean, he won?

Josey: I am drunk.

Joyce: What!

Josey: I am drunk. I drank some beer.

Joyce: You better be glad I cannot remember how to get to your house. I hope you get sick as a dog.

Josey: I am not going to get sick. I feel good. (I could tell she was upset by the way she spoke to me.)

Joyce: Let me tell you what is going to happen to you if you start back to drinking.

She reminded me of all the unclean spirits that had left my body before I was filled with God's spirit.

Matt 12:43-45: "When the unclean spirit is gone out of a man, he walketh through dry places, seeking rest, and findeth none. 44Then he saith, I will return into my house from whence I came out; and when he is come, he findeth it empty, swept, and garnished. 45Then goeth he, and taketh with himself seven other spirits more wicked than himself, and they enter in and dwell there: and the last state of that man is worse than the first. Even so shall it be also unto this wicked generation." (KJV)

Joyce told me I had better pray and ask God's forgiveness. By the time I got off the phone I was cold sober. This happened on a Saturday night. That Sunday morning I woke up with marks on my face. It looked as if I had been in a fight. When Joyce saw me she asked what had happened to my face. I told her maybe one of the demons got mad because she prayed me sober. I said maybe they got mad because they did not get the opportunity to get back in their old house. At the time I was making a joke because I was not aware of familiar spirits. I don't have long fingernails. What happened to my face is unknown, but it was enough for me to know in my heart that I will never drink again. Even though I say I will never drink again, the devil still tries to trick me to drink.

During the Christmas season (1998) I was in a

store that sold alcohol, and I found myself standing in front of the beer and wine coolers. I didn't realize it in the beginning, but I was standing there trying to justify drinking. The conversation I was having with myself went something like this. "Where in the Bible does it say I cannot drink? Jesus drank wine. (John 2:1-9) It only has a little bit of alcohol in it." This little conversation went on for about five minutes. I finally understood what was happening. The devil was trying to help me justify drinking. I laughed out loud at him and then I started to pray in the spirit. This has happened to me on other occasions. There have even been times I could taste and smell alcohol when none was in sight. But I have God's spirit to help me whip that little alcoholic demon who feels he can take control of my mind by tricking me into drinking.

One other incident when the enemy tried to trick me into drinking occurred while working in a nursing home. We sometimes give some of the patients non alcoholic beverages. On this particular night I decided to drink a can of beer; after all, it was non-alcoholic (a trick of the devil). I drank one can and it tasted really good. After work I stopped by 7-Eleven and bought a six-pack. After I had emptied my third can, I decided to read the label. (I should have read the label before I started.) The label showed that there was a small percentage of alcohol in the beer. I began praying in the spirit because I realized I had been tricked. I needed the power of the Holy Spirit to keep me from drinking the other three cans. Acts 10:34: "God is not a respecter of persons."

God's spirit is where we get our power. When the enemy attacks my body, praying in the spirit is the only way I can get relief sometimes. One night as I was experiencing a great deal of pain in my feet and legs, I started to pray in the Spirit. When I opened my eyes I saw what appeared to be a woman at the foot of my bed. She was rubbing my feet. When I saw this I quickly closed my eyes again. I was not afraid, but I did not believe what I was seeing. I kept my eyes closed for a short period. When I opened my eyes again she was still there rubbing my feet. After this time, I closed my eyes and went to sleep. When I told Stella what happened she explained to me what ministering spirits are. Ministering spirits are a gift to us from God to protect and comfort us against the power of evil spirits. Hebrew 1:14: "Are not all angels ministering spirits sent to serve those who will inherit salvation?"

Sidebar: I know that God sends us

ministering angels, but not like that. I would have passed out if I woke up and found someone massaging my feet. I actually would have broken out fighting and screaming. God knows my heart and I am glad he has not allowed me to see anything spiritual or feel any demonic spirits. I am sure I will in time when it is necessary.

When I finally went back to church, I enjoyed the message, but I had a problem with the praise and worship. The pastor sang one of her long songs. I said to myself, "Why does she have to sing so long?" As soon as the thought left my mind it seemed as if she stopped singing. The pastor said, "I know some of you are thinking why it takes so long for me to worship the Lord. Let me tell you why." At that point I said, "Oh Lord, did you tell her what I said?" I was ashamed because I believed that God had told her what I said. After that I made up my mind that I would praise and worship the Lord however long it takes. As for the whistles and the babies, I prayed that God would help me with this. The next time I went to church I noticed that being around the children did not have the same effect. God answered my prayer and helped me to overcome this area.

In all things we must take the first step; God will take care of all the things we have no control over. My first step was to buy a tambourine so I could make my own joyful noise unto the Lord. Now I understand why the pastor says "Glory to God" so much. She is thanking him for all the blessings he has given her. Now I can say "Glory to God" for her, for the word she teaches and for the church that is my home.

Something beautiful happened during the service on this particular Sunday. About halfway through, a still, quiet voice said to me, "You are safe now." I felt a sense of peace come over me like I had never felt before. I knew from that word that I would never leave the church again unless God moved me.

Chapter 17
ANGELS WATCHED OVER ME

Psalms 91:11: "For he shall give his angels charge over thee, to keep thee in all thy ways." Thank you, Jesus, thank you, Jesus, was all I could say New Year's Eve morning as I looked in my bed at the utility knife that was lying there. The blade of the knife was fully extended and pointing upward. As I sat on the bed I was trying to understand how I had slept on a knife without being stabbed or cut. I said, "God! How is this possible?" How could I lie on the knife without feeling it? How did the knife get in my bed? Two days later I was still thanking God for protecting me when I heard a voice say, "Write the book."

I said, "Write the book?"

He said, "Write about your life."

I said, "God, I'm not a writer."

He said, "Write the book!"

I knew I had to obey, so I started to write. The following day God showed me the cover of the book. I was standing on a railroad track watching my mother as she walked away. Standing by me was Jesus holding my hand. What I saw was exactly what I remembered happening to me 45 years ago when my mother gave me away. The only difference between what God showed me and what actually happened is I did not see Jesus holding my hand. I told Martha what God had shown me. A few days later she brought me the cover of a church program. The title on the program was, "I have taken you by the hand and kept you." The picture on the program was of a black woman holding a small child. This was my confirmation that God had inspired me to write about my life.

The Holy Spirit gave me the courage and confidence to begin writing. As my life began to unfold before me, there were times when I begged God not to reveal some things to me because, as the memories began to return, I felt a sense of fear about what I might see. Nevertheless, with the encouragement and prayers of my friends, I had the strength to finally accept whatever was brought back to my remembrance. God started me down the road of my life by getting me to accept and release some things about my life that I have held onto for 47 years. God's words to me were:

Yes, you were abused.

Yes, you were neglected.

Yes, you are a product of your environment.

Yes, you went through hell; however, you didn't have to stay there as long as you did.

The revelations he gave me to help me understand the road I had traveled was a vision of a highway. The highway led to heaven. Along the highway are many exits. These exits lead to destruction. When I exited the highway, I always had the option of coming back on immediately, but I chose to continue down the road of destruction. Matthew 7:14: "But small is the gate and narrow the road that leads to life and only a few find it." God has allowed me the opportunity to view the pleasures of the world (sin). The longer I stayed in sin the more I saw and the more I sinned. No matter what I did or where I went, Jesus was there to lead me back as soon as I would make up my mind to give up the worldly ways. At times, as soon as he led me back, I would get off again at the next exit. Jesus didn't give up on me. He kept leading me back to the right path over and over again.

Ezek 34:11: "For this is what the Sovereign Lord says: I myself will search for my sheep and look after them. [12]As a shepherd looks after his scattered flock when he is with them, so will I look after my sheep. I will rescue them from all the places where they were scattered on a day of clouds and darkness. [15]I, myself will tend my sheep. [16]I will search for the lost and bring back the strays. I will bind up the injured and strengthen the weak."

Chapter 18
THE NURSING HOME

One day as I was driving to work I noticed a Red Cross building. I have passed this building for two years without ever giving it a thought, but on this day as I passed the building I made a decision to become a Red Cross volunteer. Little did I know that God had plans for me. I had prayed for several months for God to use me to help people physically and spiritually. I never planned on working in a nursing home. Old people were not on my list of people to like. As a matter of fact, I didn't even like being around them. As I walked into the office, my plan (not God's plan) was to work with babies. Jeremiah 29:11: "I know the plans and thoughts I have for you, saith the lord, thoughts of peace, and not of evil, to give you an expected end."

After speaking with the director of the Red

Cross, I was told they needed friendly volunteers at the nursing home. I said I would give it a try. On my first visit to the nursing home I was shocked at what I saw. It was a room filled with elderly people who had Alzheimer's. I left the nursing home thinking, Oh my God, I can't do this? But the next day I went back. I said, "Lord, if you want me to do this you will have to help me." I began to realize that God had given me what I had asked for. I wanted to take care of babies and he did give me babies. The only difference with these babies is that they were very old.

My first patient was a gentleman who was very mean and very strong. He would fight the nurses and the staff. The first time I saw him was during a fight with the nurses. They were trying to get him to go into the dining area to eat. He would not let them near his chair. I told the nurses to leave him with me and I would take care of him. I prayed for him to accept me. The first thing I did was to rub his back, which I thought would relax him. After a few minutes of this I could feel the tenseness go out of his body. When I asked him if he was ready to go inside he said, "Yes." I learned quickly that he responded when you touched him and spoke softly to him. After about two months of working with him he began to flirt with me by patting me on my rear end whenever

I got in reach of him. He may have had Alzheimer's, but he still remembered what a woman was. I guess there are some things you just never forget, even in old age. He was eventually moved to another nursing home and started all over again to be mean to the nurses, but he was never mean to me.

After a few months of volunteering, I began to have doubts about what I was doing. One night as I prayed I said, "Lord, I know we are not supposed to ask you for signs and wonders, but I am not sure if I am in the right place. If you want me to continue to work in the nursing home, wake me up at 3:00 in the morning as a sign for me to stay." The very next morning at precisely 3:00 a.m., I woke up and my spirit told me to look at the clock. I looked at the clock, laughed out loud, and gave God thanks for showing me exactly where I was supposed to be. When I told my friend what happened, she asked me if I had prayed out loud. I told her no. I knew only that God had awakened me at the time I asked him to. I also knew he was the only one who could help me.

I didn't have a problem with the clean patients, but I would avoid the ones who looked a little unkempt. For instance, one day a man sat next to me and his nose was running. He used his hand to clean his nose. I slid my chair away from him. Each time I moved my chair away from him, he would move his chair closer to me. I finally said, "Lord, do you want me to talk to this man?" No answer. I said, "Lord, his hands and nose are nasty." No answer. I pulled my chair over a little and the man pulled his chair over too. Finally, the answer dropped into my spirit. Acts 10:34: "God is no respecter of persons." I turned around to the man and said, "Mr. Johnson, do you want something?" He said, "Yes I do. I lost something and I am trying to find it." I asked him, "What did you lose?" He said, "I lost Jesus." I was shocked because I had never heard this man speak. He said, "Can you help me find him?" We talked for a while; then I led him into confessing the sinner's prayer (Romans 10:9-10). When I finished he got up and walked away. A few minutes later he came back to me and said, "Thank you, miss. Thank you so much." I don't remember ever seeing this gentleman again. After this incident, I got me a big box of Wet Ones. If they needed it, I would clean their nose, hands, or whatever needed to be cleaned and forgot about their appearance. God, and only God, conditioned me to see the person and not the person's appearance.

Jill is not her real name, but she was a patient whom I intentionally stayed away from. She appeared to be the most depressed and withdrawn person in the unit. I didn't know how to approach her. She would sit and stare at me while I was talking to the other patients. For some reason she intimidated me. She would look at me as if she dared me to get close to her. The look in her eyes was evil. To really be honest about it, I was afraid of her. I had heard that many of the people in nursing homes have demons in them. I knew what God's words said about it. 1 John 4:4: "Greater is he that is in me than he that is in the world." But I also knew Acts 19:16: "And the man in whom the evil spirit had leaped on them, overcame them, and prevailed against them, so that they fled out of that house naked and wounded." At this point I was thinking more about the second verse than I was the first. I just stayed away from Jill. I had no intentions of getting close to her, but that was not in God's plan.

One Sunday after I left church my prayer to God went something like this. "God, I am going to the nursing home. You can use me any way you desire. Lead and guide me to the persons you want me to talk to. Help me to know and say the right things to them." The one thing I forgot to say was, "Lord, I'm afraid of Jill so don't lead me to her." I don't remember how or why, but I found myself sitting next to Jill. I began to pray by saying, "Lord, do you want me to talk to her?" I knew the Lord had placed me next to her because there was no way I would have placed myself next to her. Therefore, I was sure he would help me if she went in to her attack mode. I had already seen how she would attack the nurse and I had heard the sounds she would make. The sounds were like those of an animal. After I realized God had directed me to her I felt a sense of peace come over me. I said, "Hello, Jill, how are you today?" She did not respond, but I continued to talk to her, still failing to get a response. When she finally looked at me, I touched her. She looked confused at first; then she began to relax. I didn't know what to do next so I started to pray in my prayer language. I prayed so only she could hear me and as I prayed I held her hands in mine. I noticed a peaceful look come upon her face, so I continued to pray and finally there it was—a big smile on her face. I had never seen her smile before, so with that encouragement, I continued to pray. She took my hand in hers and said, "Thank you." I could not believe she had spoken to me. She said it again as I got up to leave and as I walked away from her, tears of joy fell down my face. I can still remember the touch of her frail hands because when she touched my hands, she also touched my heart. I thanked God because I knew in my heart that God had allowed me to reach her through her spirit man.

Later, as I was about to leave she said, "Get a bed in my room so you can stay with me." When she made that remark about me staying with her I said silently to myself, "Oh no God, don't put me here." I said, "Jill, I love you but I can't stay here." She said, "You are the only person who loves me." I told her that God loved her and she said, "I don't think so." Many of the people in the nursing home do not feel that God loves them because their family has deserted them. Jill said, "If God loves me, why would he put me here?" I explained to her that nursing homes are for people who can no longer take care of themselves. I told her that God sent me to the nursing home to take care of her. She looked at me, smiled, and said, "Well, that was nice of him." I also told her about God's word in Deut. 31:6: "Be strong and of a good courage, fear not, nor be afraid of them: for the Lord thy God, he it is that doth go with thee; he will not fail thee, nor forsake thee." As 1 said before, Jill's mind was clear sometimes and other times she would forget.

One day I told her I wanted her to remember two things even if she couldn't remember anything else. The first one was the name of Jesus, and the second thing was to remember my name. I told her if she ever needed me Jesus would let me know. She said, "You're going to be sorry you told me that." I did not understand what she meant at the time, but a few days later I was sitting at my desk at work when I heard my name being called over and over again. At first I thought I was going crazy. I looked around my office, but no one was saying anything. I asked the man behind me if he had called me and he said no. I then began to realize it was Jill's voice I heard. I told my boss I had to leave. The nursing home was about five minutes from my job. When I got to the nursing home and entered Jill's room the nurse standing beside her bed said, "Boy, am I glad you're here." She said Jill had been calling my name for the last hour. I hurried over to the bed and asked Jill if she was all right. She looked up at me with a big old smile and said yes. I asked her why she was calling my name. She said she just wanted to see if I was telling her the truth. I asked her what she meant and she said, "You told me if I needed you, Jesus would let you know. So, I wanted to see if it was true." All I could do was laugh. I had made the statement about Jesus letting me know she was calling to make her feel good. I never knew she was going to test it.

The next day when I visited her she said, "Jesus" just as I walked in the door. I was so happy that she could still remember Jesus' name. I said, "Jill, I am so proud you remembered what I said. Now tell me what my name is." She said, "I don't remember." I told her that I was a little hurt that she did not remember my name. She looked at me and said, "Your name is not important." I could only laugh. She remembered the name that was above all names, and that was the most important thing to me.

Over the next two years Jill and I fell in love with each other. She got so sick they had to take her to the hospital to be treated. She was in the intensive care unit for a while. I knew that it was getting close to the time for her to leave this world and to go be with the Father. When God decided it was time to take her home I did everything I could to keep her here. I prayed, I begged, and pleaded with him not to take her. I told him that Jill was the only person who loved me. "Why are you taking her away? Please don't take her. Let her stay a little while longer." I sat with Jill in the hospital every day for five weeks. I would tell her about God and her new life. Rev 21:21: "The twelve gates were twelve pearls, each gate made of a single pearl. The great street of the city was of pure gold, like transparent glass." I wanted her to know about the streets that were paved with gold and the walls that were covered with all kinds of jewels, and the gates made of pearls; she would have her very own mansion and she could travel as fast as she wanted to go. One day I told her what the "Word" says about us having a new body. She asked what was wrong with the body she had. I left that question alone. I asked her if she was ready to go home and she said yes, but I realized she wanted to go home with me. I also realized that I had to let her go. So, I prayed to God and asked him that if he was going to take her, please don't let her die in the hospital. I asked him to let her get well enough to go back to the nursing home so she would be with all of the people who loved and cared for her. I asked him to let her die in a place where she would not be alone.

Two days later they sent her back to the nursing home. Once she returned, I started to prepare her for her new home. When she said she was ready to go, I told her to tell God. She said, "God, I'm ready." I began to pray for God to take her and as I was praying for her I said to myself, "Jill, I wonder if you can still smile." It was hard for me to remember the last time I saw her smile. I said to myself, "When I finish praying, I will ask her to smile for me." But as soon as I finished the thought, Jill started to laugh out loud. I was shocked again. In the two years we were together I only heard her laugh a couple of times. She rarely smiled at all. I looked at her as she laughed and I knew in my heart that only God could do such a beautiful thing. A few days later I walked into her room expecting to find her sitting in the bed looking beautiful, but she had a peculiar look on her face. I should have realized her time was up because I had seen this look on other patients' faces before they passed, but it just did not register at the moment. It finally dawned on me that this was a look of peace. There are no words to explain the beauty on a dying person's face who is at peace with God. As I was leaving I told her she was my best friend. Her voice was very weak, but God allowed me to hear her say, "You are my best friend too." That night my best friend died in her sleep.

At her memorial service I met her family. I had never seen them before. As the people stood up to say words of kindness and to share memories of her life, I learned that Jill had volunteered at a nursing home prior to her becoming ill. I also learned that her best friend was a black woman whose name was Josephine. This was really a weird coincidence, but I could believe that. The pastor said that God had given me to Jill as a gift. He said Jill had served and helped many people when she was well, so I was given to her to make her last days easy. My personal prayer to God was, "Dear God, when I am old, let someone be there for me. Do not let me leave this world feeling bound by my environment. Bless me, Father, as I have blessed others. In the name of Jesus I ask these things. Amen." I thanked God for the strength and the love that he placed in my heart to work with the elderly. Many people ask me how I can go there and work with those old crazy people. I tell them it is easy because I know what it's like to be bound and helpless. I know what it is like not to receive a hug or a kind word. I know what it feels like when there is no one who cares whether you live or die. Knowing all these things, I can relate to the hell they are going through by being left alone to die. I also tell them that if it was not for the Holy Spirit, I could not go near a nursing home. Several of the nurses could not understand why the people responded to me the way they did. I always told them it was not me, but the Holy Spirit that dwells within me that made them accept me and the kindness I had to offer them. It was strange to them because they did not believe in the Holy Spirit.

Matt 13:13-16: "Therefore speak I to them in parables: because they seeing see not; and hearing they hear not, neither do they understand and in them is fulfilled the prophecy of Esaias, which saith, by hearing ye shall hear, and shall not understand; and seeing ye shall see, and shall not perceive. [15]For the people's heart is waxed gross, and their ears are dull of hearing, and their eyes they have closed; lest at any time they should see with their eyes, and hear with their ears, and should understand with their heart, and should be converted, and I should heal them. [16]But blessed are your eyes, for they see: and your ears, for they hear."

I thank God for blessing me with a special gift. God allowed me to give love to people who meant nothing to me prior to my meeting them. God also allowed the patients to teach me a few meaningful lessons. It took the words and remarks of the patients to make me realize how blessed I really was.

One day while I was talking to one of the patients, I was not aware that I was complaining about something. The patient looked at me and said, "Why are you complaining? You can leave here anytime you get ready. I have to stay here for the rest of my life." On another occasion I was complaining about the elevator not working. The building had five floors and I wasn't in any mood to walk that far. A patient in a wheelchair said to me, "Why don't you walk up the stairs? You have two good legs." I began to realize how I sounded to the patients. God later gave me this word of knowledge. One morning as I arrived at work, God dropped these words into my heart. "Stop complaining and thank God for what you do have." As I thought about these words I realized that I started my day off complaining. I complained about having to get out of bed. I could be homeless and sleeping in a box or handicapped and unable to get out of bed. I complained about going to work. I know how it feels to be without a job and not have a savings account. When I got to work I complained about the people I had to work with. I complained about the food I ate. Perhaps I should try fasting for a week or so. I complained about the weather. I complained about things I have no control over. Some of the things I complained about are blessings from God, but I was so busy compiling I couldn't see it as a blessing. I purposed in my heart, from that day forth, not to complain again. The first thing I say each morning when I wake is "Thank you, God, for letting me wake up." The next thing I say is, "God, give me the strength to get out of this bed." I thank God I have a job to go to, a roof over my head, and plenty of food to eat. I try to utilize the time I spend complaining giving God thanks and praises for all that he has done for me. Rather than cursing the people I work with, I pray for them. It is much easier to pray than complain. I even thank God for the weather. It does not matter if it is raining or if the sun is shining. For whatever day it is, it is the day that the Lord has made and I shall rejoice and be glad in it. I still complain sometimes, but I know with God's help one day I will stop complaining altogether. My prayer to God is that he will keep me from complaining about the many things I have no control over. God has allowed me to be in this situation so that he can be glorified by the results. When I was on the verge of suicide, the Lord sent an old acquaintance to me to get me to go to church and to give my life to him. I will be forever grateful for his mercy and grace.

According to Webster's dictionary, complaining means to express feelings of dissatisfaction, resentment, or pain. When we complain we are saying, "God, I am unhappy with what you are doing. This is the day that you have made, but I elect not to rejoice and be glad in it." We waste a lot of time while we are in the world serving the devil. We are happy with all the things we have, but we don't realize we are losing our soul.

Chapter 19
SHARING THE WORD

While taking a break during my volunteer duty at the nursing home, a young lady sitting at the table next to me started to talk about how strange the weather was. Her conversation opened a door for me to share what the word of God has to say about "There will come a time when we will not know one season from another." I was grateful for the opportunity to share the word of God with her. Break was over and I was preparing to leave when the words came out, "Ask her if she is a Christian." I felt a little foolish even though I love sharing the word of God with others. I had never outright asked anyone if they were a Christian. This time I did exactly what the Holy Spirit told me to ask her. I said, "Are you a Christian?" She lowered her head and said, "Yes I am, but I am a backslider. I did something bad." I asked her what she did. She said that she had called a psychic hotline and ever since that day her life had been a living hell.

My break was over, but I told her I would bring her what the word of God said about witchcraft. Lev 19:31: "Regard not them that have familiar spirits, neither seek after wizards, to be defiled by them: I am the Lord your God. The soul that turneth after such as have familiar spirits, and after wizards, to go a whoring after them, I will even set my face against that soul, and will cut him off from among his people." A few days later I had the opportunity to speak with her again. I gave her all the information I could find about her situation. As we spoke she informed me that she also went to a palm reader. I told her that calling a psychic hot line and going to a palm reader were not things that God approved of. "However, he loves you and all you have to do is repent and ask for his forgiveness."

1 John 1:8-10 NIV): [8]If we claim to be without sin, we deceive ourselves and the truth is not in us. [9]If we confess our sins, he is faithful and just and will forgive us our sins and purify us from all unrighteousness. [10]If we claim we have not sinned, we make him out to be a liar and his word has no place in our lives."

She said, "I pray every night." I said, "But you have not repented." I didn't even know why I said that. Nevertheless, she admitted that she had never repented. As I continued to speak I realized it was not my words that were going forth to her, because some of the things I was saying I would have no knowledge of. I knew it was the spirits speaking through me. I do not remember everything I told her, but I remember telling her she had allowed evil spirits to enter her. I also said that she had placed a curse on her son by the evil thing she had done. I told her to pray and ask God to cover her and her son with the blood of Jesus. I said, "God wants you back, but you must repent and never do what you did again." Acts 3:19: "Repent ye therefore, and be converted, that your sins may be blotted out, when the times of refreshing shall come from the presence of the Lord." As I was speaking she began to shake and she said, "What is that? What is happening?" I thought it could be the Holy Spirit or it could be demons fleeing. About an hour later I saw her again and she told me she had repented. She said, "I don't have to be on my knees to repent, do I?" I said, "No, you do not have to be on your knees." However, I did explain to her why we pray on our knees and why we lift our hands to praise God. 1 Timothy 2:8: "I want men everywhere to lift up holy hands in prayer, without anger or disputing."

A few months later she told me one night she suddenly woke up in the middle of the night. When she looked at her son, who was in bed with her, she noticed his eyes were rolled back in his head. She did not tell me what was wrong with the child. She said, "I am a nurse but I could not remember what to do. I could not even remember how to dial 911. All I could do was call on Jesus, and after calling on Jesus I remembered what I had to do." She told me she knew that it was the Holy Spirit that woke her up. She said, "If I had not woken up, my child would be dead." The lesson I learned from this situation is that we must always be prepared to witness to anyone God leads us to. There are many backsliders in this world who believe God will not forgive them for things they have done. Those that make it to church can receive the words of wisdom and knowledge through Bible study, the lessons, and the pastor's sermons, but what about those who have no pastor? We must be ready to speak the word of God at all and any time. "Son of man, I have made you a watchman for the house of Israel; so hear the word I speak and give them warning from me." (Ezekiel 3:18) "When I say to a wicked man, 'You will surely die,' and you do not warn him or speak out to dissuade him from his evil ways in order to save his life, that wicked man will die for his sin, and I will hold you accountable for his blood. [19]But if you do warn the wicked man and he does not turn from his wickedness or from his evil ways, he will die for his sin; but you will have saved yourself." Just like Ezekiel, all Christians are responsible for sharing the word by witnessing whenever the opportunity presents itself.

As I shared what I knew about communicating with familiar spirits and the people who take advantage of others by making them believe they have the answer to life's problems, I saw a look of shame and fear come upon her face. I told her about God's love and forgiveness. She looked at me as if I was a mother telling her child a bedtime story. I could see the change on her face. The lesson I learned from this situation was to advise people that the psychic hotline will open your spirit to demonic activity. Once you give a demonic spirit a right to oppress or possess your body, he has a right to stay.

James 4:7: "Submit yourselves, then, to God. Resist the devil, and he will flee from you." The devil's temptations may seem overwhelming at times, but the Bible teaches that if we submit to God, we have the power to not only resist, but drive away the devil entirely.

Luke 18: "¹And he spoke a parable unto them to this end, that men ought always to pray, and not to faint." Romans 12:12: "¹²Rejoicing in hope; patient in tribulation; continuing instant in prayer." Ephesians 6:18: "¹⁸Praying always with all prayer and supplication in the Spirit, and watching thereunto with all perseverance and supplication for all saints." Colossians 4:2: "²Continue in prayer, and watch in the same with thanksgiving." 1 Thessalonians 5:17: "¹⁷Pray without ceasing."

This individual I ministered to was a Christian who had no idea that calling a psychic hotline, using Ouija boards, going to palm readers, meditating on heavy metal music, playing Dungeons and Dragons, and using any form of magic or witchcraft could change her life forever. Television commercials use celebrities to entice people into calling those 1-800 numbers. Most people figure if a famous person endorses a product, it must be good. If you want to know if it is right or good, check the Bible first. If it's not in the word of God there is no need to waste your time or money on it. I explained to her why we do not communicate with familiar spirits. I told her about God's love and forgiveness. I could see the expression of relaxation and peace come upon her face as I told her about how much God loves us and how forgiving he is. God allowed me to give this person a truth, with revelation knowledge, that she will be able to pass on to someone else. Many people who use their gift of knowledge, fortune-telling, and prophecy for psychic hotlines and the palm readers have been given a gift by God, but they use it for evil.

Acts 16: "Once when we were going to the place of prayer, we were met by a slave girl who had a spirit by which she predicted the future. She earned a great deal of money for her owners by fortune-telling. [17]This girl followed Paul and the rest of us, shouting, 'These men are servants of the Most High God, who are telling you the way to be saved.' [18]She kept this up for many days. Finally Paul became so troubled that he turned around and said to the spirit, 'In the name of Jesus Christ I command you to come out of her!' At that moment the spirit left her.

[19]When the owners of the slave girl realized that their hope of making money was gone; they seized Paul and Silas and dragged them into the marketplace to face the authorities. [20]They brought them before the magistrates and said, 'These men are Jews, and are throwing our city into an uproar [21]by advocating customs unlawful for us Romans to accept or practice."

Psychics and palm readers use their ability to

connect with the spirits that belong to people. This is how they know so much about a person whenever they are giving a reading. God intended this gift to be used for the edification of the body of Christ. Psychics use their gifts to make money, thereby defiling God's gift. This places them on the dark side, tuned in with the devil to do the work of the enemy. " John 10:9-11: "⁹I am the gate; whoever enters through me will be saved.[a] He will come in and go out, and find pasture. ¹⁰The thief comes only to steal and kill and destroy; I have come that they may have life, and have it to the full.

¹¹"I am the good shepherd. The good shepherd lays down his life for the sheep.

"I am the gate; whoever enters through me will be saved.[a] He will come in and go out, and find pasture. ¹⁰The thief comes only to steal and kill and destroy; I have come that they may have life, and have it to the full. ¹¹"I am the good shepherd. The good shepherd lays down his life for the sheep."

They are in tune with the devil and their sole purpose is to make money; this pleases the devil. These things also open up your spirit to demonic spirits.

One of the things I have learned about the devil is that if you do his bidding he will reward you. But the price you have to pay is not worth the reward, unlike

God, who gives to us freely. Because God gives to us freely we are to follow in his footsteps. The following inserts are messages that God gave to me. I wish to share them with you.

6 April 1996 0730   *Word of Knowledge*

My children, how can I give to you when you refuse to take? How can I love you when you refuse to accept? How can I prevent you from going to hell when you insist on going? Open up your hearts and I will give you the desire of your heart. Let your eyes and heart be your guide. Let no man mislead you for I am the way, the truth, and the light. Keep my commandments and you will enter the gates of heaven. Be good to your brothers and sisters. Teach them my ways, deny no man the knowledge you have, and share everything; love, money, home, and friends. I am the way, the truth, and the light, no man will enter heaven except by me. Thus said the Lord. So be it. Amen

19 February 1999

Tell the people how much I love them.

Tell them how I have taken care of you over the years.

Tell them I have no desire for them to go to hell.

Tell them to accept me as I have accepted them.

Tell them to reach out for me. I am waiting, for it is my desire that none shall perish. I am the way, the truth, and the light. Come unto me, my children, for your rest, for in hell there is no rest. Thus said the Lord

The joy and peace of heaven are everlasting and the torment of hell is everlasting. Decide today which one you choose. For I am the Lord your God. Choose me and choose life. Live, my children live.

Chapter 20
WITCHCRAFT, GEORGE, and UNGODLY SPIRITS

(As told by Josey)

I was shocked as I walked in the door of the nursing home. In the center of the lobby someone had placed a fake graveyard. As a matter of fact, the whole nursing home was decorated to look like a graveyard. To me, this was the same as inviting the devil right into your mind and body. When I reported to my station I was asked to give out cookies and drinks. One of the men who was blind ate his cookies very fast. Before I could leave his area he said, "Lady, give me some more cookies." I told him I couldn't give him any more because the remainder of the cookies was for the ladies. I jokingly told him the men get two cookies but ladies get six. He said that was unfair. I told him that ladies should always get more than men. We went back and forth with this conversation for a short period. I finally gave him more cookies and decided to sit with him awhile. After sitting and talking for a while he began looking up at the ceiling. I think I mentioned earlier that George was blind. He said, "What are they doing?" I looked up in the direction he was looking and said, "What is who doing?" He said, "Why are they just sitting around?" I followed his eyes and said, "George, what are you talking about?" He said, "Don't you see those people?" I said, "No, what people?" He said, "Stop playing. There are people sitting all around this room." I asked him, "What do they have on?" He said, "They have on black and gray dresses or pants." He went on to say, "One man has on an army uniform." I felt George was just making up the story so I forgot about it for a while. It finally dawned on me that George was actually seeing spirits so I immediately stopped that conversation and started to talk about something else.

We talked about the weather for a while and then he started to look up at the ceiling again. He said, "Now they are drinking, but they are not talking. No one is talking." I said, "George, what else do you see?" He said he saw a cat. I asked him what color the cat was. He said the cat was black. Well, that was enough of that conversation for me. There was no doubt in my mind that decorating the nursing home for Halloween brought in and unleashed something unnatural into the nursing home. George was not making up that story. He was looking around the room as if he could actually see. When I left the nursing home that night I said, "God, please don't let any demons follow me home." Sometimes I would forget to pray before I went to bed at night. During the night I would have to get up from my bed to pray because of the unfamiliar noises I would hear in my room. At times I could feel the presence of something in the house. I was not sure what it was, but I knew it was not the presence of God, so I would get my oil out and anoint my body and my home. I was a new Christian. I was not aware that you only needed a very small amount of oil. I would pour the oil all over my house. One day as I was leaving the house I noticed the oil dripping from my door. When I told my friend Joyce, she laughed and told me that I only needed a little oil. It is what the oil represents that matters, rather than the amount used. The way I figured it, the more oil you poured on the quicker the demons would go.

There was a time when I didn't believe in demons; however, volunteering in the nursing home has allowed me to see them in action. I have seen them tormenting the patients. On two separate occasions I have had one speak to me. On another occasion I had finished work and was leaving the home when I heard a lady yelling as loud as she could, "Help me, help me, help me." I went into her room with a sense of urgency, not really knowing what to expect. She said, "Help me make them stop. Please take me home with you." I told her I could not take her home with me. I started to pray for her. She stopped yelling and looked at me. She said to me in a different tone of voice, "Stop that, I don't need that." I continued to pray silently. I tucked her into bed and told her everything was going to be okay and not to worry about anything. That night in a dream I saw demons running from my room. The next day as soon as I got on duty, I went to see the lady who had been screaming for help. She had died that night around the same time I had the dream. I was told she died in her sleep. Most of the people in the nursing home no longer know how to pray, even though they were Christians before they lost their memory. The devil takes advantage of them because they can no longer pray. He believes they are going to heaven so he torments them because they are helpless.

Chapter 21
HOLY-GHOST-FILLED, TONGUE-TALKING, BIBLE-CARRYING CHRISTIAN

I felt so blessed my head started to swell. I believed I was something special because God had chosen me to do a special work. I lost focus because of all the wonderful things that I was doing and forgot who was to be glorified. If you know anything about God, you know that he is a jealous God. He will not allow you to forget him or take his glory away. This is what happened when my head got too big:

I had a collision with the rod of God. God hit me harder than I can ever remember being hit. He showed me something about myself that I was not aware of. I have always felt that I was an honest person, at least to myself, but God has shown me that I have un-forgiveness hidden in my heart. Now, some of you who read this book might say, "He's right," but before you judge me, hear me out. We can always see the faults in others but not in ourselves. We all say we don't hate anyone, but do we love everyone? There is no in-between; you either do or you don't. The time has come for God's people to clean up their temples. If you don't clean it he won't want to use it. God has a calling on my life but I cannot do what is expected of me until I clean all the dirt out of my temple. The dirt of my temple is blocking the doorway to my heart. God has allowed me to see miracle after miracle. He has allowed me to receive and give love to others that might never have the opportunity to receive love again. When I first went to the nursing home I asked God why he had sent me there. He said, "So that you may receive and give love." He later told me I was there to witness to the sick, their family members when they came to visit, and all the staff. After I obtained this information I began to feel really spiritual, but God showed me the dirt in my temple. He then gave me the cleaning tool, which is the Word of God.

Chapter 22
GOD'S MESSAGE TO ME ABOUT
UN-FORGIVENESS AND LOVE

God used Jesus as his example to me. 1 Corinthian 15:5: Cephas (Peter) was the first apostle to see the risen Lord. We can only marvel at the grace of God in granting such a blessing to one who did not seem to deserve it. Peter's witnessing of the resurrection was a sign of his personal restoration to fellowship with Christ. It also confirmed his appointment by God to serve as a leader in the emerging church.

True forgiveness is when you can hug a person after you have forgiven them. True forgiveness is trusting a person after you have forgiven them. God used Jude and Peter to show what true forgiveness really is. We are all striving to be like Jesus. Speaking forgiveness out of our mouth is not always from the heart. If you really want to know if you have forgiven a person who you feel has wronged you, give them a great big hug. It will let them know that you are really sincere about forgiving them and starting all over again. If you don't forgive people, God can't forgive you. Do not block any of your blessings or anything you need to receive from God by not forgiving your brother or sister. I know it is hard to forget what happened and it will take you awhile to put it behind you, but you must do it in order to succeed. Mark 11:24-26: "Therefore, I say unto you, what things so ever ye desire, when ye pray, believe that ye receive them, and ye shall have them. [25]And when ye stand praying, forgive, if ye have ought against any; that your Father also which is in heaven may forgive you your trespasses. [26]But if ye do not forgive, neither will your Father which is in heaven forgive your trespasses."

A lot of people have been in church for years not receiving answers to their prayers and missing out on God's blessings because they hold things against their brother and will not forgive them. You must realize that it is only hurting you and your family, not the person you have not forgiven. If you can think of anyone you need to either forgive or ask their forgiveness, take a moment to write their names down right then because you may forget later. When you get to a telephone, or to their house, stop by or call and tell them that you have held forgiveness from them or that you need their forgiveness for whatever offense occurred. Most of the time it has been so long since the offense occurred, the people have probably forgotten all about it. Just tell them anyway that you forgive them or ask forgiveness. Don't ever give anyone that much control over your life. Because you won't forgive them, you are being held hostage because the Lord cannot forgive you as long as you hold it. Let it go and free yourself. Pray to the Lord and ask him to cleanse you of all un-forgiveness and receive your liberty, right then and there. If you don't know where they live anymore, or if they have passed just tell the Lord that you forgive them wherever they are. This will save you a lot of stress, headaches, and heartaches.

Chapter 23
THE MIRACLES OF GOD

One of the most memorable things that ever happened to me in the nursing home was one day I sat beside one of the patients who did not speak, but she understood when you spoke to her. She looked at me and began moving her mouth as if she was speaking. At first there was only a sound; however, as she moved her lips I began to understand what she was saying. She said, "Since you have been here things have changed. The people come and go, but they do not care about us. You are different because you really do care about us." Then she asked me if I understood her and I said yes. I think she asked me if I understood because I was looking in her mouth trying to figure out how I understood what she was saying when there were no words coming out. I recalled saying to myself, "My God, how did I do that?" I realized I did not do anything at all on my own, but it was God who did it.

There are many miracles performed in nursing homes, hospitals, and jails every day, but we don't see them because we are not there. God showed me that he can make the blind see and can make a person speak who no longer speaks. He also showed me that he could make me understand what was being said even though no words were coming out of the woman's mouth.

I thank God for all the miracles I have seen in the nursing home. I also thank him for not letting me see what George saw on that Halloween night. I personally do not think I would have benefited from seeing what George saw anyway and I am grateful I didn't. I know that God knew he would have to carry me back to the nursing home if I had seen what George said he saw. Thankfully, God knows my strengths and my weaknesses. Viewing the dead sitting around a wall drinking is not one of my strengths.

Chapter 24
KNOW YOUR ADVERSARY AND LISTEN WHEN THE HOLY SPIRIT SPEAKS

Once I made up my mind that I would never leave the Church again, the battle started. I had no idea how angry I had made the devil. He was so mad, he tried to kill me. Sometime during the first week of December Stella called me at home. This was unusual because Stella never called me at home. When I answered the telephone she said, "Josey, are you okay?" I said, "Yes." She said, "Are you sure?" I said yes. I asked her why she had called me. She just said that I was on her heart and she wanted to make sure I was okay. When we ended the conversation I thought about the call. As I stated before, she never calls me at home. I normally call her. I have always believed that Stella is my earthly guardian angel because she always knows when something is wrong, even when

I try to hide things from her. No matter how cheerful I try to sound, she knows when something is wrong just by listening to my voice.

I could not stop thinking about why she called me. I called her back a day or so later. She told me that she was cleaning and God had laid me on her heart. As we were speaking she said, "Let me read you something." She began reading to me from her daily word. For the seventh of December it talked about knowing your adversary and his tricks. For the eighth it talked about listening to the Holy Spirit. A few days later as I was lying in bed I heard a voice say, "I will protect you, I will protect you." This phrase was spoken to me at least three times. Approximately three days later I was making a picture frame when I heard a voice say, "Close the knife." I looked at the utility knife that was lying on the table. The knife was open, but it was in the middle of the table. I continued to work and I did not close the knife. I was told a second time to close the knife. I failed to obey the second time. A few minutes later the knife flew off the table and into my hand. I looked at my hand and all I could see was white meat. The knife had cut through several layers of flesh. I grabbed my hand and yelled out loud, "Jesus, by your stripes I am healed." I wrapped my hand because I thought there would be blood. I checked my hand a short time later to find that there were only a few drops of blood on the cloth I had wrapped my hand in.

The next day at work some of my coworkers asked me what happened to my hand. I told them about the knife, but I did not tell them about the voice I heard. Some people indicated that I was going to get an infection. What they did not realize was I had prayed and my hand was healing as we were speaking. The doctors say that because I am a diabetic, wounds are not supposed to heal quickly. The wound from the knife was totally healed in three days. What was so amazing about this incident is that it was easy for people to see any infection resulting from the cut. But it was hard to see the hand healed in three days.

Chapter 25
DON'T LOOK AT ME, LOOK!

On 20 May, 1999 I was reading an article about child abuse. As I was reading I saw the words "Hidden Bruises." When I looked at those two words God's spirit told me to go back to my word processing program. I didn't even think why, I just returned to the program and all of a sudden I started to write the following words:

Don't look at me and think I'm fine
I have been molested several times.
Don't look at me and expect me to be sweet
I was raised and raped on the streets.
Don't look at me and wonder why
I have no desire to live, I want to die.
Don't look at me and say my life is a shame
I don't even know my real name.

Don't look at me and expect me to smile
I've had to travel many miles.
Don't look at me and feel sorrow
For God has promised me a new tomorrow.

Look at me now, yes, I'm fine
For God has blessed me for all my bad
times.
Look at me now, yes, I'm sweet
For now I bless the people on the street.
Look at me now; you don't have to wonder
why,
For you can tell that this is God's gift from
on high.
Look at me now, I am not ashamed
For Jesus has given me a brand-new name.
Look at me now, expect me to smile
For God has given me joy that stretches for
miles.

"DON'T LOOK AT ME. LOOK!"
Written by Josephine Knight-Knell and the
Holy Spirit
May 20, 1999 at 13:00 p.m.

When I looked at the title of the poem, I realized

what it meant. It meant for you not to look at me because of the way I was. Look at me the way I am. Don't continue to see my faults that were wrought during my past; look at the accomplishments that I have made up to now. When people look at people who are mean and evil, all they can see is the person. They rarely take the time to find out why the person responds the way they do.

Stella was the first person who did not look at me the way I was. She looked at me for what I could become. She took the time to go to the Source (God) to find out how she could make a difference in my life. When Stella and I talked about our friendship she told me when she looked at me she saw a rock, but as she continued to LOOK she saw a diamond under the rock. She took the time to chip (pray) and chip away at the rock until she reached the diamond underneath. She did not reach her goal overnight, but she did not give up on me. In fact she continued to pray for me to make sure I stayed polished. She knew that even a diamond needs cleaning every now and then.

Throughout the Bible we can see how Jesus looked, saw, and beheld situations. He did not look at what the person was; he looked at what the person was to become. People can only see the outside, but God can see what is in our hearts. Taking the time to share Jesus with others is a Christian duty. The following words of knowledge are a message God gave me when I first started my Christian walk

Exodus 20:2-17 ² "I am the LORD your God, who brought you out of Egypt, out of the land of slavery.

³ "You shall have no other gods before [a] me.

⁴ "You shall not make for yourself an idol in the form of anything in heaven above or on the earth beneath or in the waters below. ⁵ You shall not bow down to them or worship them; for I, the LORD your God, am a jealous God, punishing the children for the sin of the fathers to the third and fourth generation of those who hate me, ⁶ but showing love to a thousand {generations} of those who love me and keep my commandments.

⁷ "You shall not misuse the name of the LORD your God, for the LORD will not hold anyone guiltless who misuses his name.

⁸ "Remember the Sabbath day by keeping it holy. ⁹ Six days you shall labor and do all your work, ¹⁰ but the seventh day is a Sabbath to the LORD your God. On it you shall not do any work, neither you, nor your son or daughter, nor your manservant or maidservant, nor your animals, nor the alien within your gates. ¹¹ For in six days the LORD made the heavens and the earth, the sea, and all that is in them, but

he rested on the seventh day. Therefore the LORD blessed the Sabbath day and made it holy.

¹² "Honor your father and your mother, so that you may live long in the land the LORD your God is giving you.

¹³ "You shall not murder.

¹⁴ "You shall not commit adultery.

¹⁵ "You shall not steal.

¹⁶ "You shall not give false testimony against your neighbor.

¹⁷ "You shall not covet your neighbor's house. You shall not covet your neighbor's wife, or his manservant or maidservant, his ox or donkey, or anything that belongs to your neighbor."

If we can learn to live by these words, the world would be a better place to live in. We should learn to give God praise and Glory for his mercy and goodness to us. You may not be aware of this but the Lord really does gives his angels charge over us to keep us from dangers seen and unseen. I know he has spared my life several times. I wonder how many times he did it that I don't know about. He is an awesome God who looks out for us when we don't have sense enough to look out for ourselves. If you are bored and want something to do, read the 91ˢᵗ Psalm to find out just how much God loves you.

Chapter 26
EPILOGUE

When Josey told me she was going to write a book, I was really glad for her. I told her it would be good therapy. I knew she had some problems that she wouldn't talk about. I became closer to her through Christ than I did while we were serving together in the United States Army. She was a very smart person who attended all kinds of schools. I told her she should publish her book because it would be a blessing and a witness to other people who have been molested, abused, or mistreated. Sometimes it helps to know that you are not the only one who has been through some terrible things but made it anyway. As she wrote each chapter she would bring it to me to find and correct any mistakes made. Once she really got serious about the writing, she decided to get a professional editor to get the book "publish ready."

Starting with chapter one, she would bring it by the store so that we could pray over it before mailing it out to the editor. On Thursday, 17 June, 1999, Josey called me at 3:00 and told me she had finished chapter three and was ready to mail it. She said she would be getting off work at 4:00 p.m. and would be here by 4:15 because she did not work too far from the boutique.

At 3:45 I received a call from Josey's job. Her supervisor asked if I was her contact person in case of an emergency. I told him I was. He said Josey was found slumped over on her desk and that the ambulance had just left to take her to the hospital. He said I should go there to meet her. I hurriedly locked the door to the boutique and rushed to the hospital, which was about 15 minutes away. When I got there I saw her supervisor standing in the waiting area right across from the emergency room. When I got close enough to see his face, I knew things were not good. He told me that Josey was dead before they got her to the emergency room. I was in shock. I could not believe what I was hearing. The last time I saw her, which was the day before because I saw her every day, she did not look sick.

It took a while before we could bury her because we had to wait for her husband to sign for the release of her body to the funeral home and then wait until he came from Germany for the actual funeral. It took about two weeks for everything to be over. She told me the devil was trying to kill her before she turned 50, but he couldn't do it. Only God has the power to give life and to receive a life back to himself in his time and season. She lived to be 53 years old on this earth but she will live eternally with the father in heaven.

I was just thinking back to some of the things Josey told me, and I must add this note to her book. She said when she was small, her father denied she was his daughter. She never really knew him because his wife forbid him from seeing her. His wife hated her because every time she saw Josey it would re-mind her of his infidelity. From what I understood, she had two or three half brothers from her father's marriage. They were not allowed to even speak to Josey. When her father died, they contacted Josey to come to his funeral. She did not want to go but decided that it was the right thing to do. She had a hard time forgiving him for not owning her. She be-lieved her life would have been a whole lot different if she had been welcomed into that family. I forgot the name of the town where they lived; I even forgot the name of her father and brothers. She stayed in a hotel while she was there. The day she arrived she was contacted by a lawyer. He set an appointment for Josey to come see him. To her surprise, her father had left the house they lived in to her. Can you imagine that? The lawyer gave her a letter from her father saying how sorry he was that he never owned her as his daughter. Giving her the house was supposed to make up for all those years that she was denied.

It was a good thing that Josey was now a Christian. She said her first thought was to put his wife and half brothers out in the street, but she did not do that. I think the arrangement she made with the wife was that she could stay in the house as long as she paid the taxes every year and that she sent rent to her. I don't know how much it was. When she died, I don't think her father's wife was notified of her death. I wonder how long it took them to discover that she was dead. I know they did not show up for her funeral.

I wonder sometimes how her life would have been different if she'd had kids and a family who stood beside her. None of that matters now because she is finally home with the real father. She often told me that she wanted to "whoop" the devil for stealing so much of her life. I was telling her that you can't fight him like that. Ephesians 6: (The Armor of God) "Finally, be strong in the Lord and in his mighty power. [11]Put on the full armor of God so that you can take your stand against the devil's schemes. [12]For our struggle is not against flesh and blood, but against the rulers, against the authorities, against the powers of this dark world and against the spiritual forces of evil in the heavenly realms. [13]Therefore put on the full armor of God, so that when the day of evil comes, you may be able to stand your ground, and after you have done everything, to stand. [14]Stand firm then, with the belt of truth buckled around your waist, with the breastplate of righteousness in place, [15]and with your feet fitted with the readiness that comes from the gospel of peace. [16]In addition to all this, take up the shield of faith, with which you can extinguish all the flaming arrows of the evil one. [17]Take the helmet of salvation and the sword of the Spirit, which is the word of God. [18]And pray in the Spirit on all occasions with all kinds of prayers and requests." With this in mind, be alert and always keep on praying for all the saints. With His armor on, you will have a chance to win the battle.

I always tell young women that they should not miss the joy and fulfillment of having children. It makes a lot of difference when you get old. You can always count on your children to look out for you and take care of you, if you have raised them right. Josey

ad no family here so she had to rely on the supposed friendships she had built since she arrived in
Virginia. I don't know how, but her supervisor had a
key to her apartment. Since she died at work he probably got it with the rest of her personal effects left in
the office. She had not known him for that long, but
she did think he was trustworthy. While Josey was
doing all of that shopping in the thrift stores, she was
purchasing antique Tiffany lamps, beautiful antique
baskets, and other valuable antique tables and chairs.
I want it to be known that he stole a lot of those items
before he gave the key to her best friend, who came
from out of town. I wanted to make note of this fact
just in case he purchase this book. I pray to God that
he finds himself in this book as a thief that preyed on
an innocent person who trusted him. I wish I had the
foresight to hang onto her key, but I was not thinking
straight.

When her best friend Stella arrived, she took everything else that belonged to Josey. I was given her
purse when I left the hospital, but I gave that to Stella
also. I wish I had kept it. I ended up with nothing be-
longing to Josey except her obituary. When I went to
her apartment everything was gone except a box of
trash that was sitting in the middle of the floor. Just
before I left the apartment the Holy Spirit directed

me to look in the box of trash. In it were the original sheets of her book that I had corrected. I was actually glad they had discarded her testimony. Well, I guess that is not exactly true. Her friend took her computer, almost new, which had all of her personal stuff and her book on it. I wonder if it was important enough to her to keep. From what Josey told me about her best friend it did not convince me that she was a real true friend.

Josey was married to a German guy, but they were separated. He was an alcoholic, but I believe he loved her at the time. She was ashamed to go out with him because she really didn't want anyone to know she was married to him. Before she left to come back to the United States she took all of the clothes she had bought for him and cut them up. She wanted to make sure he wasn't going out on dates in any of the clothes she bought him. After she became a Christian she wanted to reunite with her husband, but he did not want to come to the United States. She said she would never marry again and she would not date anyone because she realized she loved her husband. He was the beneficiary of a nice-sized insurance policy. He did come to the States to her funeral, but he could not wait after the funeral to go to the burial ground. I resented him for that, but there was nothing I could do about it. I know Josey truly loved him. I hope he realized that.

I know you have read some things in this book that are hard to believe. That is your choice, but I do believe that this book is ordained of God to tell the world of his goodness and to let you know that no matter what, you are never alone. I know she is looking down from heaven saying something crazy like, "Too bad they are stuck down there." She often talked about being in heaven and now she has finally arrived. I look forward to meeting my old friend again. I want to be able to tell her about how many lives she touched through this book of her precious memories and experiences. I love you, Josey.

Breinigsville, PA USA
08 September 2010
245001BV00004B/1/P